STARTING OVER

The Making of John Lennon and Yoko Ono's

Double Fantasy

STARTING OVER

KEN SHARP

With Photographs by Roger Farrington
and David M. Spindel

GALLERY BOOKS   VH1 BOOKS

NEW YORK LONDON TORONTO SYDNEY

Gallery Books
A Division of Simon & Schuster, Inc.
1230 Avenue of the Americas
New York, NY 10020

First VH1 Books/Gallery Books hardcover edition October 2010

GALLERY BOOKS and colophon are trademarks of Simon & Schuster, Inc.

For information about special discounts for bulk purchases, please contact Simon & Schuster Special Sales at 1-866-506-1949 or business@simonandschuster.com.

The Simon & Schuster Speakers Bureau can bring authors to your live event. For more information or to book an event contact the Simon & Schuster Speakers Bureau at 1-866-248-3049 or visit our website at www.simonspeakers.com.

Designed by Joy O'Meara

Manufactured in the United States of America

10 9 8 7 6 5 4 3 2 1

Library of Congress Cataloging-in-Publication Data is available.

ISBN 978-1-4391-0300-5
ISBN 978-1-4391-6926-1 (ebook)

Charles Shaar Murray article found on pages 197–198 courtesy of Charles Shaar Murray and *Mojo* magazine.

Dedicated to the memory of John Lennon
and my beloved basset hound, Herman

Contents

CONTENTS

Introduction

December 8, 1980, 10:30 p.m.

John Lennon is on top of the world. *Double Fantasy*, the music icon's first new album in five years, has just been released and is heralded as a triumphant artistic comeback, marking the artist's celebrated return to the top of the music charts. "(Just Like) Starting Over," the album's first single, is warmly embraced by rock radio and becomes a smash number one hit.

Ensconced inside New York's Record Plant, Lennon's just finished the mix on a new Yoko Ono song, "Walking on Thin Ice," which he excitedly predicts "will be Yoko's first number one record." Saying a quick good-bye to producer Jack Douglas, Lennon and Ono exit the studio onto the darkened streets of New York City. They hop into a private limo, which takes the couple on a short drive back to their home at the Dakota on West Seventy-second Street. Minutes later Lennon will be shot dead at the hands of a crazed assassin.

Shortly after 11:00 p.m., *Monday Night Football* sportscaster Howard Cosell breaks the tragic news to a stunned nation that Lennon has been killed. With news of Lennon's senseless murder, *Double Fantasy*, his final musical statement, rockets to number one around the world.

Rewind to 1975 . . .

Retiring from the music world in 1975, after the birth of John and Yoko's son, Sean, on October 8 (also John's birthday), the former Beatle bade farewell to life as an internationally renowned rock star and spent the next half a decade happily living his life out of the media spotlight, spending his time as a "house husband," raising Sean, baking bread, and writing the occasional song.

During that self-imposed five-year retirement from the music world, Lennon was the source of intense media scrutiny. Pundits endlessly speculated about how such a revered musical icon could disappear altogether and transform into a real "nowhere man." Yet freed from the shackles of contracts and unyielding public and critical expectation, Lennon felt free for the first time in decades. No longer under the media microscope, he retreated to embrace his family life and recharge his creative batteries.

In the summer of 1980, a June trip to Bermuda found Lennon newly inspired to write and record once again. With an Ovation acoustic guitar in hand and two Panasonic boom boxes set on "record," he composed many of the songs that would form the basis of *Double Fantasy* and the follow-up posthumous release, *Milk and Honey.* These include "Nobody Told Me," "Borrowed Time," "I'm Losing You," "Woman," "I Don't Wanna Face It," "Beautiful Boy," and "I'm Stepping Out."

Soon, plans were set in motion for a new album by John and Yoko. Enlisting producer Jack Douglas (Aerosmith/Cheap Trick/Alice Cooper) and a seasoned studio band numbering guitarists Hugh McCracken and Earl Slick, bassist Tony Levin, drummer Andy Newmark, and keyboardist George Small, the troupe entered New York's Hit Factory during the first week of August 1980 and over the next few months Lennon and Ono worked steadily on their new record.

The music world had changed dramatically since the release of Lennon's 1974 album, *Walls and Bridges*, his last studio album of original material. By 1980, the new wave/punk sounds of the Clash, Talking Heads, Elvis Costello and the Attractions, and Blondie dominated the musical landscape. Pink Floyd's concept album *The Wall* was hailed as a masterpiece while Tom Petty and the Heartbreakers' third album, *Damn the Torpedoes*, ushered them into superstardom. Lennon's first album in five years was highly anticipated by critics and the public, though many openly wondered how the eighties zeitgeist would impact the new record.

Signed to David Geffen's new label, Geffen Records, on November 17, 1980, John and Yoko's *Double Fantasy* was unveiled to the world. Save for a flash of anger powering the track "I'm Losing You," this is a kinder, gentler Lennon, his songs a celebration of domesticity and love. Gone was the primal scream howl of *Plastic Ono Band*, the political proselytizing of *Sometime in New York City*, or the blue heartbreak that seemed to engulf *Walls and Bridges*. No longer an angry young man nor a rebel with a cause, Lennon at forty reveled in the contentment of his family life. His clear adoration of his son, Sean, was elegantly expressed in "Beautiful Boy." Yoko also found her voice as a solo artist. For the new album, with songs like "Kiss Kiss Kiss" and "I'm Moving On," she crafted a batch of her most accessible songs, which still managed to retain her trademark experimental flair.

With Lennon's new single, the retro-sounding Elvis–Roy Orbison hybrid "(Just Like) Starting Over" racing up the charts and talk of a tour in 1981, it looked like Lennon's amazing comeback was a fait accompli. Sadly, his tragic assassination less than a month later at the hands of a deranged fan silenced the musical legend, but his music lives on.

Starting Over: The Making of John Lennon and Yoko Ono's Double Fantasy documents the extraordinary tale behind Lennon's last album. The book is constructed as an oral history told by the album's key principals, including Yoko Ono, producer Jack Douglas, engineers, arrangers, the entire studio band, Geffen Records honcho David Geffen, key record company personnel, music journalists, photographers, and Lennon himself via archival interviews. Together they serve to weave a comprehensive portrait of Lennon's last days. Augmenting the text are scores of previously unseen images of John and Yoko in the recording studio taken by photographers David M. Spindel and Roger Farrington. The intimate and candid photos capture John and Yoko on the first day of recording the *Double Fantasy* album and showcase images taken the last day a photographer was permitted to photograph them in the studio.

Almost three decades since its release, *Double Fantasy* is recognized as one of music's most seminal and beloved albums. For the first time ever, *Starting Over: The Making of John Lennon and Yoko Ono's Double Fantasy* offers an account behind the creation of that historic record, which would ultimately serve as John's last musical statement.

Cast

John Lennon

Yoko Ono

Jack Douglas (producer)

David Geffen (owner, Geffen Records)

Ed Rosenblatt (president, Geffen Records)

Hugh McCracken (guitar)

Earl Slick (guitar)

George Small (keyboards)

Andy Newmark (drums)

Tony Levin (bass)

Rick Nielsen (guitar, Cheap Trick)

Bun E. Carlos (drummer, Cheap Trick)

Howard Johnson (baritone sax)

Arthur Jenkins Jr. (percussion)

Eric Troyer (background vocals)

Tony Davilio (arranger)

Lee DeCarlo (engineer)

Julie Last (assistant engineer)

Jon Smith (assistant engineer)

James Ball (assistant mix engineer)

Steve Marcantonio (engineer, "Walking on Thin Ice" session)

Rabiah Seminole (studio receptionist, the Record Plant)

Kishin Shinoyama (album cover photographer)

Bert Keane (national promotion director, Warner Bros. Records)

Bob Merlis (publicity director, Warner Bros. Records)

Annie Leibovitz (photographer)

Bob Gruen (photographer and friend)

Paul Goresh (photographer)

Stan Vincent (Jack Douglas's business partner)

Jay Dubin (director, *Double Fantasy* recording session video shoot)

Ritchie Fliegler (sound engineer, *Double Fantasy* recording session video shoot)

Andy Peebles (disc jockey, BBC Radio One)

Dave Sholin (national music director and interviewer, RKO Radio Networks)

Ron Hummel (producer/engineer, RKO Radio Networks)

Laurie Kaye (scriptwriter and co-interviewer, RKO Radio Networks)

David Sheff (music writer, *Playboy*)

Robert Christgau (music writer, *Village Voice*)

Charles Shaar Murray (music writer, *NME*)

John Swenson (music writer, *Creem*)

Jon Young (music writer, *Trouser Press*)

Bill King (music writer, *Atlanta Constitution*)

Watching the Wheels

After years in the spotlight, by the time Lennon's *Rock 'N' Roll* album hit record stores, he was burned out and desperately needed to take a break. As it turned it out, that break would be a long one . . . five years.

John Lennon: Making music was no longer a joy. For twenty years, I had been under this pressure to produce, produce, produce. My head was cluttered. Every time I'd sit down to write, there would be a cloud between me and the source, a cloud that hadn't been there before. I was trapped and saw no way out. Everything was crazy. I realized that I wasn't making records for me anymore, but because people and record companies expected me to. Still it was hard for me to admit that I was allowing some illusion to control me. After all, wasn't I the great pop seer? Hadn't I written "The Dream Is Over"? Was I not the great John Lennon who could see through all the world's hypocrisy? The truth was I couldn't see through my own. It's easy to see thy neighbor and say, "You and your phoniness." The trick is to see your own. Finally, Yoko said, "You don't have to do it anymore. You exist outside of the music." I was shocked. I had never thought of that. That was a frightening concept for me. My whole security and identity was wrapped up in being John Lennon the pop star. Could the world get along without another John Lennon album? Could I get along without it? I finally realized that the answer to both questions was yes.[1]

Yoko Ono: He knew he existed outside of music, I didn't have to tell him, but it was a nice reminder. He was trying to tell people, "Listen, you thought that I was not doing anything for five years but I was doing a lot, just not anything to do with music." A lot of guys now understand that wisdom that they could be at home and bring up a child and that they wouldn't lose their dignity by doing that.

John Lennon: I'd been under contract since I was twenty-two and I was always "supposed to." I was supposed to write a hundred songs by Friday, supposed to have a single out by Saturday, supposed to do this or that. I became an artist because I cherished freedom—I couldn't fit into a classroom or office. Freedom was the plus for all the minuses of being an oddball! But suddenly I was obliged to the media, obliged to the public. It wasn't free at all! I've withdrawn many times. Part of me is a monk, and part a performing flea! The fear in the music business is that you don't exist if you're not at Xenon with Andy Warhol. As I found out, life doesn't end when you stop subscribing to *Billboard*.[2] For five years, I'd been so locked in—the home environment—and completely switched my way of thinking that I really didn't think about music at all. My guitar was sort of hung up behind the bed, literally.[3] Musically my mind was just a clutter. It was apparent in *Walls and Bridges*, which was the work of a semisick craftsman. There was no inspiration, and it gave off an aura of misery. I couldn't hear the music for the noise in my own head. By turning away, I began to hear it again. It's like

Newton, who never would have conceived of what the apple falling meant had he not been daydreaming under a tree. That's what I'm living for . . . the joy of having the apple fall on my head once every five years.[4] When I wrote "The Dream Is Over" [in 1970], I was trying to say to the Beatles thing, "Get off my back." I was also trying to tell people to stop looking at me because I wasn't going to do it for them anymore because I didn't even know what the hell I was doing in my own life. What I realized during the five years away was that when I said the dream is over, I had made the physical break from the Beatles, but mentally there was still this big thing on my back about what people expected of me. It was like this invisible ghost. During the five years, it went away. I finally started writing like I was even before the Beatles were *the Beatles*. I got rid of all that self-consciousness about telling myself, "You can't do that. That song's not good enough." Remember, you're the guy who wrote "A Day in the Life." Try again.[5]

Bob Gruen (photographer and friend): While he was taking the five-year break, I often wondered if he would ever return to music. He didn't seem to need it. He seemed quite comfortable at home with Sean and enjoying his personal freedom. He seemed to enjoy not being in the public eye. He was in a very happy place. He came back when he was ready.

John Lennon: When I took the break I never had any time limit in mind. I wanted to be with Sean the first five years, which are the years that everyone says are the most important in a child's life. When he was coming up on five, Yoko and I thought maybe it was time to record again.[6]

Yoko Ono: I had some songs and John had some songs, but we didn't have that many. When he was in Bermuda and I was here in New York I said to him on the phone, "Why don't we make an EP?" In those days there were records called EPs. But then I got thinking and just told him, "Let's do a full album." And the minute I said, "Let's do it" he got so inspired and started to write so many beautiful songs. It was great. All I had to do was say "Let's do it" and it took off from there. John and I both inspired each other very much. I'd write "Let Me Count the Ways" and I called him in Bermuda and said, "Listen, what do you think about this?" And then I'd play it to him. Then sometime later he'd call me back and say, "Listen, just after you sang 'Let Me Count the Ways' it inspired me to write something," and he played "Grow Old with Me" and it was just fantastic.

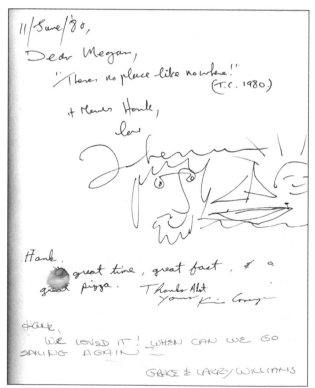

The boat log Lennon signed on his boating trip to Bermuda, where he penned most of the songs on *Double Fantasy.*

John Lennon: It inspired me completely. As soon as she would sing something to me, or play the cassette on the phone, within ten or fifteen minutes, whether I wanted to work or not, I would suddenly get this song coming to me.[7] I was in Bermuda in a disco . . . upstairs they were playing "Rock Lobster" [by the B-52s] . . . I called her [Yoko] on the phone and said, "There's a group called B-52s and there's somebody doing your act" . . . I said, "Listen to it, they're ready for you this time, kid."[8]

Bob Gruen (photographer and friend): [The B-52s] are big Yoko fans. They were inspired by Yoko to make that undulating vocal sound. When John heard it and found out it was a hit, he realized this new generation was more open to hearing Yoko's music and perhaps it was time to come back and make a new record.

John Lennon: On October 9, I'll be forty and Sean will be five and I can afford to say, "Daddy does something else, as well." He's not accustomed to it—in five years I hardly picked up a guitar. Last Christmas our neighbors showed him "Yellow Submarine" and he came running in, saying, "Daddy, you were singing . . . were you a Beatle?" I said, "Well, yes. Right."[9]

An Offer I Can't Refuse

Jack Douglas served as an assistant engineer on Lennon's *Imagine* album and also worked with Ono on two of her solo records, *Approximately Infinite Universe* and *Feeling the Space*. In 1980, a chance meeting with the former Beatle would land Douglas the producer's chair on John and Yoko's new recording project.

Jack Douglas (producer, *Double Fantasy*): I ran into John at a health food store restaurant over on the East Side about six months, maybe a year before we did *Double Fantasy*. In comes John, Sean, and the nanny. They were coming from swimming lessons at the YMCA. I hadn't seen John in years. He comes up and goes, "Hey, Jack, how ya doing?" He wanted to know what's happening and gave me his private number, which I never called. I didn't want to bother the guy because he was raising his family.

Secret Sessions

Lennon's reemergence onto the music scene would remain a closely guarded secret, enshrouded in a James Bond-like saga of mystery and intrigue.

Jack Douglas (producer, *Double Fantasy*): I got these instructions; John wants to talk to me about making this record, "Don't say anything to anyone. Just go to Thirty-fourth Street, get on a seaplane, and come out." I got flown to the big house out in Glen Cove. The seaplane landed right onto the beach. It was hush-hush. I knew I was being asked to do a record because I had already gotten the phone call from Yoko and John. I came out and Yoko handed me an envelope marked "For Jack's ears only." Inside was a cassette of all of John's demos. She and I went into the house and she handed me a stack of her songs, dozens and dozens of songs. She'd been in the Record Plant recording demos with Elephant's Memory. Then Yoko said, "John's gonna call you now." He was still in Bermuda at the time. He told me he felt he couldn't write a song anymore and that these songs were really shitty. Even the cassette itself was narrated by John. Each of the songs started out with John saying, "Here's another one, the same old crap."

Stan Vincent (Jack Douglas's business partner): Jack brought John's demo tape to my beach house in Montauk (near the Hamptons, on Long Island). That's the first time we heard it. If Jack liked this tape and thought we could make a record, John would come out of retirement and fly from Bermuda to New York to do this album. If Jack didn't think it had merit, then the record would not be made. So Jack pulls the tape out and hands it to me. I said, "Jack, we're gonna love this cassette, aren't we?" And Jack being Jack goes, "Well, we have to listen to it first." (laughs) So we put the tape in and we both flipped out. Our jaws dropped open. It was the most amazing stuff. All the material was there, "Beautiful Boy," "Woman," "Nobody Told Me."

Jack Douglas (producer, *Double Fantasy*): The other funny thing about the cassette was at the end of some songs he'd say, "Just give this one to Ringo."

Stan Vincent (Jack Douglas's business partner): When we were listening to the demos, I remember quite clearly John spoke right before "Nobody Told Me" and said, "This one's for Mr. Starkey [Ringo Starr]." That song was perfectly typecast for Ringo. I think Ringo would have a smash with that song today.

Jack Douglas (producer, *Double Fantasy*): The feel and intimacy of the demos was so great. I thought, how can I even beat the cassette? Afterward I got a call from John, who asked me what I thought of the material and I told him that it was incredible. I told him the same thing, "I don't know if I can beat this stuff, it's so good." And he cracked up.

Stan Vincent (Jack Douglas's business partner): There was a meeting set up between Yoko and I at the Dakota at Studio One. She said she didn't want any lawyers and just wanted to discuss it with me and she wanted me to draw up an agreement between our production company, Waterfront Productions LLC, and John and Yoko. So I show up for the meeting in T-shirt and jeans. I walk into Studio One and Yoko comes down and says, "Okay, follow me." I follow her and this tall thin gentleman in a three-piece pinstriped suit comes out of nowhere and follows me in. Yoko says to me, "Oh, by the way, this is David Warmflash, he's an attorney but he's a personal friend." I told her that would be fine. She specifically said to me, "Listen, I don't want to interfere with this album, this is John's baby, this is John's album." I said, "Whatever you guys want, we'll do the best that we can do." We had a good meeting and went over all the deal points. I asked her where she wanted to do the record, and she said, "You can do it anywhere in the world except for the Record Plant [because at the time she was having some problems with Roy Cicala], and no California." That was because of his "lost weekend" in California. So Jack and I decided to do the record at the Hit Factory.

Jack Douglas (producer, *Double Fantasy*): What he made clear to me was that when I did this whole process of preproduction—putting a band together, booking a studio—it had to be done in complete secrecy because he was damned if he was gonna let the press know he tried to do a record and fell on his ass. John didn't know if he could do it and he didn't want to be made a fool in the press. If anyone found out that this was going on, the project would stop.

Jon Smith (assistant engineer, *Double Fantasy*): I was an assistant engineer on staff at the Hit Factory studios. Just a few months earlier

I'd assisted on the Rolling Stones album *Emotional Rescue*, which was, I thought at the time, about as big a project as one could get. When the *Double Fantasy* project was booked in, it was originally listed under the name Rich DePalma. We'd look in the schedule book every now and then to see what was coming up and suddenly this project comes in under the name Rich DePalma and for some reason nobody would tell us who he was. It was a big secret. We felt the name sounded familiar for some reason but no one was talking. I found out later that while Rich DePalma's name sounded familiar, it wasn't. He was John and Yoko's accountant and he worked in their office.

One day I got called down to Eddie Germano's office. He owned the studio, and he sat me down and said, "I'm going to tell you something now and you cannot repeat this to anybody! Nobody must know. If anyone finds out, I'll know that you told them. Understand?" I told him I did and asked, "What's up?" He said, "Remember when you worked with the Stones, we all said, 'It doesn't get any better than this'? Well, it's about to get better than that because this project that's coming in is the first new record by John Lennon and Yoko Ono in five years." And I flipped out. So he gave me some details about when we were going to start and what we'd need to do to get ready, and he again made me swear an oath of secrecy. I left his office in a daze. Everyone knew why I'd gone to talk to Eddie and they could tell by my grin that I now knew who the mystery artist was. "Well, who is it?" they all wanted to know. And I could not tell anyone. Not a soul.

Julie Last (assistant engineer, *Double Fantasy*): When Jack put together his team for the album he invited me to be a part of it. I had worked with Jack Douglas as his assistant engineer on a number of records at the Record Plant. I had just been hired as a staff engineer at another studio when I got the call from Jack. He did tell me who the artist was, but I was sworn to secrecy. I had to ask for a leave of absence from this new position and say, "I can't tell you why, but trust me, I wouldn't ask if it wasn't really important." Guessing games and intense pressure ensued, but I kept my promise.

John and Yoko flanked by studio band. L-R: George Small, Jack Douglas, George Young, Hugh McCracken, Tony Levin, Andy Newmark, Earl Slick, Howard Johnson.

Meet the Band

Landing the plum role as producer on Lennon's comeback album, Jack Douglas began the task of assembling a studio band and recording team.

John Lennon: All the ones I used to work with were sending messages. I felt bad, but I didn't want to go back in the same bag, you know. I heard from Jesse [Ed] Davis and Klaus [Voorman] . . . I wanted to start really brand new.[10]

John Lennon: All the musicians for the whole sessions, every one of them was picked the same way [numerology or astrology].[11]

Stan Vincent (Jack Douglas's business partner): I got a call that they all needed to submit their birth dates to Yoko before they could be hired, including *my* birth date and Jack's. Everybody passed the test, thank the Lord (laughs).

Jack Douglas (producer, *Double Fantasy*): Every person that I picked for anything, whether it was the band or engineers or anyone else, their birth dates had to go through Yoko. Although John didn't name any single musician he specifically wanted to use, he told me the most important thing to him was that the musicians on the date would be his contemporaries. So if John made a reference about a particular song that may have come from the fifties or the sixties, they would understand what he was talking about. He didn't want to talk to kids.

John Lennon: The only one I knew was Hugh McCracken. I said I'd like to have someone I know.[12]

Stan Vincent (Jack Douglas's business partner): Jack and I discussed some musicians and said, "Let's put Hughie [McCracken] on it. Hughie had worked with John on "Happy Xmas (War Is Over)."

Hugh McCracken (guitar, *Double Fantasy*): Stan Vincent called me to play on John's record. It was great that John was resurfacing after five years and I was excited to be involved in the project.

Jack Douglas (producer, *Double Fantasy*): Hugh's a great player. Earl Slick was playing with David Bowie and I felt we needed another guitar player who was a little wilder, a little edgier.

Earl Slick (guitar, *Double Fantasy*): I was being managed by a woman named Trudy Green. We got a phone call from Jack that he was producing a record he wanted me to play on, but he wouldn't tell my manager who it is. For some reason, the first thing that hit me was John Lennon. A few weeks before we went into the studio to record, we got the phone call it *was* John.

Stan Vincent (Jack Douglas's business partner): Then we decided on the rest of the band. I hired Tony Davilio to do the charts and arrangements.

Andy Newmark (drummer, *Double Fantasy*): I was on tour in Italy with Roxy Music in June of 1980. I recall that Jack asked Hugh McCracken what players would be appropriate for the album. Hugh said, "On drums, Ricky Marotta, Steve Gadd, or Andy Newmark." I recall the first call went out to Steve but they never heard back from him. Thank you, Steve! I don't know if they called Rick or not. All I knew was that it was my lucky day. The message they left on my answering machine was "Please call Jack Douglas's office for sessions regarding John Lennon."

Earl Slick (guitar, *Double Fantasy*): I remember getting the phone call and having all this anxiety afterwards 'cause sometimes good news comes with a lot of anxiety. It would be like someone saying, "You've just won the lottery, now you have to drive and pick up the money." You're going, "Man, I hope I don't crash the car on the way" or "I hope they're not lying to me and there's really a million dollars when I get there." So I wound myself up.

Andy Newmark (drummer, *Double Fantasy*): My wife called me in Italy and told me about the message from Jack's office. I completely flipped out in my hotel room. I was the most excited I had ever been in my life, about anything . . . ever! I don't think anyone could know how much this meant to me. I could not have been as excited at the time about working with any other artist. John was the pinnacle for me.

John Lennon: We got the bass player by default because Willie Weeks was supposed to do it. It turned out he was doing a George Harrison session and he booked for that a long time ago. Then we found Tony Levin and I'm thankful for that now. I'm sure Willie's great, but I absolutely love Tony Levin. He's really, really amazing.

He just absolutely would just pick it up and play and it would be right. You wouldn't have to discuss it. He'd get the feel of it right away.[13]

Tony Levin (bass, *Double Fantasy*): I had worked before with Jack Douglas, and had done many albums with Andy Newmark as a rhythm section and even more albums with Hugh McCracken. Maybe I assumed one of them had recommended me for the session. I still don't know, really.

George Small (keyboards, *Double Fantasy*): I got the job playing on the album through Stan Vincent who was Jack's business manager and wore a lot of hats for the *Double Fantasy* sessions. He arranged for me to audition for Jack Douglas at the Record Plant. I was told it was an audition for John Lennon's new album, so that made the night before pretty sleepless. I knew one of the things I was gonna have to play convincingly was stride-style piano like Fats Waller, where you have to play all the notes on the piano and use all the fingers on both hands. The upright piano I auditioned on was missing about a third of the keys (laughs), so it was an interesting piano to play. Right next to that piano in a very cramped storeroom was the actual mellotron that was used for *Sgt. Pepper*. Anyhow, thankfully I passed the audition. Jack told me to show up at the Dakota the next day.

Practice Makes Perfect

Before entering the recording studio, a number of preproduction rehearsals took place at the Dakota, and later S.I.R. Studios.

John Lennon: I always play the one before just before I go in again [into the recording studio]. Like I played *Walls and Bridges* just before I came in to see what state of the art I was at then.[14]

Stan Vincent (Jack Douglas's business partner): *Walls and Bridges*, the album John did prior to *Double Fantasy*, wasn't an over-the-top smash. So John was coming off a five-year hiatus with that last album not being as successful and Paul's [McCartney] career was skyrocketing and John was quite pissed about that (laughs). I had a lot of work to do in preparation for the sessions. I had to block studio time. I had to make sure union contracts were filed properly. I heard that one of the few organizations that came to John's aid when he was having immigration problems was the Musician's Union 802 and the AFM [American Federation of Musicians]. They came to bat for him. I said, "Wow, wouldn't it be befitting, John's a member of the union, let's make him the leader of the date." It's not usually done, but I made him the leader of his own date.

One thing he hated was we had tons of contracts to sign. For every session we had to submit contracts to the union and they had to be paid in a specific time. I had so many contracts and John had to sign every single one of them (laughs). I would bring stacks of these contracts in that John had to sign, which was very tedious stuff. He had to do it because he was the union leader of his own band.

Tony Davilio (arranger, *Double Fantasy*): It was a real sunny day when we arrived at the Dakota. I went with Jack [Douglas], Hugh McCracken, and George Small for the first preproduction rehearsals. I was there to write out chord sheets for the musicians and also write out any new ideas from John or Jack for the songs. I had done the original transcriptions and lead sheets of all of John's Bermuda demos prior to meeting him. Jack wanted everything copyrighted before the project went any further.

George Small (keyboards, *Double Fantasy*): The whole atmosphere was charged. It was quite an apartment. I remember walking into the wrong room and it was filled from one end to the other, three levels high, with fur coats and other clothing. I also remember the solid gold bathroom fixtures and the huge kitchen; it could have been a kitchen for a restaurant. That stands out in my mind.

Tony Davilio (arranger, *Double Fantasy*): We did the rehearsal in this room with two pianos and an amp.

George Small (keyboards, *Double Fantasy*): John would play us songs on acoustic guitar and the piano and also he'd play cassettes he made of some preliminary versions of the songs when he was in Bermuda.

Hugh McCracken (guitar, *Double Fantasy*): John played a lot of songs and they sounded great. It was inspiring to hear that he had come up with such good material. He hadn't lost anything in the five years off. John would play the piano or guitar and we'd play along and throw out some ideas. I had my own scratch pad where I'd write down ideas for guitar parts that worked. If I played something that he liked he would stop and say, "I like that" and I'd make a notation and actually write the part out on my scratch sheet. One instance when we were playing "Beautiful Boy" I came up with a guitar figure that John liked. He stopped and said, "I like that a lot, don't forget it." I wrote it down and played that same part on the record during the song's choruses.

Tony Davilio (arranger, *Double Fantasy*): We went over Yoko's tunes, but we mainly focused on John's songs. I'd heard them already and was familiar with them. He stood up with an acoustic and played many of the songs for us. That was exciting. I remember writing the chord sheets right then for "Starting Over," which we used in the studio. During that first rehearsal, Hugh and I were arguing about a chord that John was playing in one of his song. I thought it was an A chord and he thought it was an E chord. John overheard us arguing and came over and said, "Hey hey, boys, what's going on?" We asked him, "What's the chord you use on that part of the song?" He played it and Hugh and I looked at each other sheepishly and realized we were both wrong (laughs). At one of those preproduction rehearsals at the Dakota, John told us how much he wanted to record again. He was like a kid, he was very excited. He said, "I've been a house husband for the last five years and I want to get back to the music."

Arranger Tony Davilio's original handwritten chord sheet for "Starting Over."

Jack Douglas (producer, *Double Fantasy*): Later, we had formal rehearsals with most of the band at S.I.R. Studios in New York. We had charts written that I gave to the musicians so we could start working on the arrangements. At the rehearsals with the band I would sing lead, which would crack up the band. The last rehearsal was held at the Dakota, the night before the sessions. A few of us went up into the Dakota and John answered the door, "Oh, how ya doing?"—everybody big smiles—"Okay, come on in." John had tons of equipment so we just set up a couple of little amps, the piano in the living room, and we played around. As we were leaving, John stopped us and grabs me and goes, "I got one more song I want you to hear." There was a Fender Rhodes piano by the door before you left the apartment. He sat down and played "Starting Over." I said, "Where'd that come from?" I knew it was a hit single from the second I heard it. No one knew the song because we didn't have a demo of it. I said to John, "Let's start with this song." He said, "You think it'll make the record?" I said, "Make it? It's gonna be the first single. It's perfect."

First day of recording,
August 7, 1980.

Starting Over

August 7, 1980. The location: New York's Hit Factory. After a five-year absence from music, John Lennon and Yoko Ono would enter the recording studio to begin work on a new album. The album would mark Lennon's first LP of original material since 1974's *Walls and Bridges*.

George Small (keyboards, *Double Fantasy*): The Hit Factory was one of the happening studios in town.

Jack Douglas (producer, *Double Fantasy*): We chose to record at the Hit Factory because it was out of the way. The studio was located way over on the West Side at Tenth Avenue and Forty-eighth Street in a building that no one would think to camp out in front of. No one would know. We could go in and out of there without ever being seen.

George Small (keyboards, *Double Fantasy*): At the time it was considered off the beaten track so it was the perfect studio for John to do his new record and maintain a veil of privacy. They were very uptight about keeping this well under wraps. John hadn't done

anything for five years. He'd been a house husband. I don't think he wanted to be hammered by the media, "Hey, John, how did it go this morning? How did it go this afternoon?"

Stan Vincent (Jack Douglas's business partner): The Hit Factory had a private elevator that went to the sixth floor where John and Yoko would be recording. A select few had private keys for the elevator, which helped give John and Yoko some protection and privacy.

Jack Douglas (producer, *Double Fantasy*): It caused a lot of problems with the people I worked with at Record Plant because they thought the project should come there. The Record Plant was so visible. That's where they would *expect* him to be. I just couldn't do the record there. The first month we were working at the Hit Factory, no one outside of the studio knew what was going on.

Jon Smith (assistant engineer, *Double Fantasy*): We'd spent the previous day setting up the studio and getting drum sounds so we'd be all set to go when John and Yoko arrived. We sent our security man, James McClain, down to meet them at the front of the building to make sure they got upstairs without anyone harassing them, which hopefully wouldn't happen because it was a big secret that they were coming in. He brought them up to the sixth floor where the studio was and I remember John was wearing this huge hat. He walked in and he looked gigantic to me, like he was seven feet tall, which thinking back on later he wasn't that much taller than I am. Being John Lennon, though, he was such an historical figure, you couldn't help but be in awe. He came in and he was very friendly and nice. Everyone was very excited to be there, including John. It was the first time he'd been in the studio for years.

George Small (keyboards, *Double Fantasy*): According to my 1980 logbook, we did three days of rehearsals, August 2, August 4, and August 5. We started the sessions officially at the Hit Factory on Thursday, August 7 and we worked nine hours, from 2:00 p.m. to 11:00 p.m. I remember the sessions going well into mid-September.

Earl Slick (guitar, *Double Fantasy*): I got to the studio before any of the other musicians on the first day. I was like a kid in a candy store. I got there an hour earlier. I wasn't excited, right? (laughs) So I showed up at the Hit Factory and nobody was there. I walked into the main studio and John's sitting there by himself and he's got a guitar in his lap and he's just noodling around. I went to introduce myself and he said, "Nice to see you again." And I was like, "Huh? Nice to see you, too, but we haven't met." He said, "Oh yeah, we met on the Bowie *Young Americans* sessions." I said, "Trust me, if we'd worked together before, I would have remembered." (laughs)

George Small (keyboards, *Double Fantasy*): There was an electric anticipation everywhere.

Jack Douglas (producer, *Double Fantasy*): Everyone was a little nervous.

Hugh McCracken (guitar, *Double Fantasy*): I had the advantage of already knowing John and Yoko so that was helpful on the first day of recording. I was definitely psyched.

Andy Newmark (drummer, *Double Fantasy*): The band showed up the first day for proper recording at the Hit Factory. You never know what to expect with any new artists you haven't worked with, but when you freelance, that's just part of the landscape. It was very exciting that it was John Lennon, but I never lost sight of the fact that the most important thing here and now was the music we were about to make. My only concern was playing well and making the music feel good. We were there to help him make a record. For freelance studio players, this is business as usual. It just so happened to be someone who was very, very famous and someone we had a tremendous amount of respect for. You just have to jump in the deep end and get to work. John Lennon and the Beatles were a big deal in my life. Very big. The fan in me was in awe of John Lennon. I just tried my best to stay cool and focus on my drumming. Anyhow, when John showed up, he said hello, had a cup of coffee, made some small talk for a few minutes, and then said, "Okay, let me show you guys a tune." This was within thirty minutes of his arrival. I liked that. That's what we were there for, not to socialize, but make a record. He wanted to get right into it. He didn't waste any time. I loved his directness.

Hugh McCracken (guitar, *Double Fantasy*): Everything clicked right away with the whole band and John.

Andy Newmark (drummer, *Double Fantasy*): We got a track within a couple of hours, I recall. I was relieved. That's excellent for a first day.

Lee DeCarlo (engineer, *Double Fantasy*): That first day we recorded two basic tracks, "Starting Over" and one of Yoko's. We'd always alternate. We'd do a John song and then a Yoko song.

Jack Douglas (producer, *Double Fantasy*): I had Earl sitting next to Hughie. The chart for "Starting Over" was a quick scribble. I put two of them on Hughie's music stand and said, "Pass one to Earl." And Earl, of course, didn't read a note of music (laughs). No one knew Earl, he was the new kid in town. Everybody else knew each other. They were all session guys. Earl was acting like he could read it, but actually he was busking along and just listening to what everybody else was playing.

Earl Slick (guitar, *Double Fantasy*): The guys that worked on the record were seasoned session players. Hughie had played on everything from Paul Simon to the Monkees to Paul McCartney. Levin was already an established session guy. Andy started out playing with Sly and the Family Stone. They gave me some rough chords and mostly I'd look over at Hughie and say "What's this and what's that?" I was basically a loose-cannon, rock and roll guitar player. That's what John liked about me. Everybody else in the band were organized session guys who had their shit together and I was absolutely a loose cannon. I'd come into that studio hungover and beat up, but I still got it done. Hughie's style was more sophisticated than mine. Musically, he was a lot more knowledgeable than me. At that time I came from a blues-rock thing. My early influences were Keith Richards, Cream, the original Jeff Beck records, and the Yardbirds. That's where I was coming from.

Hugh McCracken (guitar, *Double Fantasy*): I thought it was a great idea of Jack's to call Earl in. He wasn't the typical studio player. The overall rapport and chemistry between us was great.

Earl Slick (guitar, *Double Fantasy*): Our styles meshed well on the record. I was playing a lot more contained than usual because the songs didn't call for me to do anything other than that.

Andy Newmark (drummer, *Double Fantasy*): I knew and was very fond of everyone in the band, having worked with all of them over the years, except for Earl and George, who I met for the first time at the start of the recording, and liked them a lot immediately. We, the players, all got on great together. No reason not to. I felt we all got on well with John right from the start and connected with him immediately.

Arthur Jenkins Jr. (percussion, *Double Fantasy*): I first worked with John on *Walls and Bridges*. Lennon came in focused, but the musicians he brought in from California weren't. They were more interested in starting off the session with what I call "amenities" rather than tuning up and getting down with the music. For *Double Fantasy*, the work experience was completely different. Lennon came in prepared to take care of the business of music. And unlike the *Walls and Bridges* experience, the band was as focused as John. We got to work immediately. He was at the top of his game. The point he made is that he still had it. He was a master artist of our time.

Tony Levin (bass, *Double Fantasy*): John came right up to me during the Hit Factory sessions and said hi in a very straightforward, New York way. Something to the effect of "They tell me you're good, just don't play too many notes." I responded, "Don't worry," knowing, as he did not know yet, that I'm the kind of player who's very happy just holding down the bottom end.

Tony Davilio (arranger, *Double Fantasy*): John wasn't familiar with Tony Levin's work before. Tony's a great player. He played everything from straight-ahead jazz to fusion to rock. And right after John heard Tony play, he thought he was great. He liked Tony and called him "Kojak" because he was bald.

Tony Levin (bass, *Double Fantasy*): Paul McCartney's bass playing had a big influence on my playing. When I approached John's music I couldn't help approach it in a somewhat Paul-like way, which wasn't that different than approaching in my own way, melodically with a big, fat bass sound. I think John occasionally hummed a bit of a bass line to me, probably early on. After a while he left them to me. I don't recall John saying anything to me about the parts, but I was flattered, later on, to hear that some of my lines had been doubled by horn section overdubs.

Stan Vincent (Jack Douglas's business partner): When I heard one of the first songs being recorded I was stunned because this band was such an amazing assemblage of super talent. Each one of the musicians that played on the album contributed to so many hits by other artists we know and love. You take that energy and put in the components of great musicians like Hughie, George Small, Andy [Newmark], Tony Levin, Earl [Slick], Tony Davilio. They could have cut songs for years and each track would have been better than the last.

Andy Newmark (drummer, *Double Fantasy*): To me, the band was into a groove right from the start. Mind you, that is what guys like us are supposed to do . . . sound really good and not take long, either. When you have players of this caliber making music, it's always going to be of a high standard. Each new track we got under our belt was another little victory. As time went on, we all understood more about what John liked and didn't like, musically speaking. So the chemistry built. As each track went by, John gave less and less instruction to us because we understood where he was coming from, and what to play and what not to play, stylistically. He began to trust our instincts. Fortunately, our instincts were never far from his. You have to have the right players for the music in any situation. John's music seemed like a very natural fit for all involved. The atmosphere kept getting more and more relaxed each day and

41

John seemed to genuinely dig what was happening. That lent to all of us really playing our best because we felt accepted and that made us relaxed. We all play our best when we are relaxed. So everything just kept getting better and better every day. Day one was really good but by day four, man, we were burning! I was really happy with what was going down. From day one, everybody seemed to give John what he wanted, musically speaking. If the boss is happy, I'm happy. Everything we did came together very quickly.

Tony Levin (bass, *Double Fantasy*): You could tell from the beginning of the sessions that John respected all of us as players and he was comfortable letting us know exactly what he wanted from the song, yet also open to things from us that he'd not planned on. From my end, using hammer-on bass chords for the intro of "Cleanup Time" or a fretless bass for the end section of "Watching the Wheels" or my whistling on a rundown of one of Yoko's songs. I think it was John who said to use that on the recording.

George Small (keyboards, *Double Fantasy*): John would get in the vocal booth and count it off and start singing. Man, that voice would be enough to galvanize you into playing in the proper spirit. I couldn't always see him, but the presence of his voice was in your headphones, it was inside your brain. I mean, there were times I just had to pinch myself, "Am I here?" (laughs) We all realized the sessions were historical and that it was ridiculously cool that we were working with him.

Andy Newmark (drummer, *Double Fantasy*): I would walk home with Hugh McCracken every night just pinching myself, going, "Hugh, am I really here? Is this going down as smoothly as it seems? Are we really in the studio with John Lennon making a record that sounds this amazing?"

Yoko Ono: The first day John and I went into the studio to work on *Double Fantasy* was a very nerve-racking day because neither of us had been in the studio for years. For both of us the nerves didn't really go away until we had finished recording all of the tracks. We finished the tracks very fast. So right after that and after hearing what we'd done, and that it was a good record, that's when we stopped feeling nervous about it.

Keeping It Quiet

News that John was back in the recording studio after a half-decade absence from music making would have ignited a hailstorm of international press interest. In order to protect the sessions from intense media scrutiny, everyone involved in the making of the album was sworn to secrecy.

Tony Levin (bass, *Double Fantasy*): I got a call at home after the first day, saying that the sessions were to be kept secret and they'd rather I didn't even tell anyone whom I was working for, let alone where. I took a taxi to the second day's session, telling him "Forty-eighth and Ninth," to give me a little fresh air walk to the midblock studio. "That's the block where John Lennon is recording," he said. I asked how he knew and he replied, "Heard it on the radio."

Lee DeCarlo (engineer, *Double Fantasy*): Tony told John the story and he just threw up his hands. "How the hell does the cabdriver know where I'm recording?"

Jack Douglas (producer, *Double Fantasy*): We were in there a month before any official acknowledgment that these sessions were going on. The tough part was keeping the staff at the Hit Factory quiet. I think Eddie Germano, who ran the studio, threatened them not to say anything. Ed knew if word got out we were doing this record we'd pull the plug on it. I'd tell the musicians that John wasn't sure if he could do it. He was very, very insecure. He didn't think he had it anymore, you know. He thought he was too old, he just couldn't write, he couldn't sing, he couldn't play, nothing. It took a while. There were some moments there where he was like, "I don't know . . ." I used to have breakfast with him every morning at 9:00 a.m. I'd come to the Dakota and he was always so punctual. He came out his door and we'd walk from the Dakota to La Fortuna on Seventy-first Street, a little cafe. We'd sit in the back garden and have chocolate iced cappuccinos and talk over what happened last night, what was gonna happen, what was going on with Yoko, everything. There were moments at La Fortuna where I had to say, "John, really, I swear, it's good. You sound great."

In the Studio

For the next month, John, Yoko, their studio band, producer Jack Douglas, arranger Tony Davilio, background singers, engineers, and scores of others were sequestered inside the Hit Factory, busy at the work at hand. The sessions would prove highly productive, with the duo cutting a collection of over twenty strong tracks. The songs would be tapped for both *Double Fantasy* and a follow-up posthumous 1984 release, *Milk and Honey*.

Eric Troyer (background vocals, *Double Fantasy*): Security was really tight at the Hit Factory. No one could get up to that [sixth] floor. There was very limited access. Yoko had a real tight control on everything.

Yoko Ono: It was an incredible time. We had this five-year hiatus where we were sitting in the Dakota, taking care of Sean, and I was taking care of the business. We decided that we wanted to spend our time doing that and not write a song. Then suddenly we were going into the studio to record and it was just a big high, you know. On that album I tried not to be too experimental and I managed that. A song like "No, No, No" was a song that wound up on my *Season*

of Glass album, that's the kind of song that I didn't put in *Double Fantasy*. I kept the songs of mine in *Double Fantasy* in the style that they would not be too far-out.

Andy Newmark (drummer, *Double Fantasy*): John had cassette demos of the tunes with just guitar or piano, and his voice. He would play us the cassette demo and then sit with the guitar or at the piano and play the tune and sing it. We would listen and eventually pick up our instruments and start playing along. Once we played it awhile, maybe ten or fifteen minutes, he'd stop playing and go into the control room and listen closely to everyone's parts. In the beginning he couldn't remember our names because we were all new people to him, so it took a week before he had our names right. I thought that was funny. He would never try to hide the fact that he didn't know my name. In typical John Lennon fashion, he actually would exploit the fact that he didn't know my name. He'd say, "Hey, drummer, do this and don't do that." He took complete charge musically, right from the first song. If something didn't sound right he'd go, "That sucks guys" or "No, no, I don't like that at all" (laughs).

Tony Levin (bass, *Double Fantasy*): I was not so surprised as impressed that when John first would sing and play a song to us, it was so complete. The form was all worked out, the lyrics were great, and the groove right there in the guitar. You just knew what to play. All you had to do was pick up your instrument and play along. That made it so easy and such a joy for all of us. Playing bass or drums in a situation like that is the easiest thing in the world. There's no searching for the right tempo, or what kind of feel it should have. It's all there for you and you just have a ball. That's the way it was with all of his songs, and I was loving it. What's not to love about suddenly being the bass player and right in front of you is John Lennon singing a John Lennon song?

Arranger Tony Davilio's date books.

George Small (keyboards, *Double Fantasy*): There was one song where nothing was gelling, although I can't remember the title of it. John took each of us aside and directed us individually. In about ten or fifteen minutes he had everyone playing just what he wanted. He took the approach like he was fixing a machine or a watch and just tuned each one of us to the parts he wanted.

Andy Newmark (drummer, *Double Fantasy*): He would tell himself off, too, if he made mistakes. He had a way of speaking that was really direct and blunt, but it wouldn't hurt your feelings at all. It's great when someone has that ability to be very honest and straightforward but, at the same time, never alienates the person being spoken to. John was good like that. I like band leaders who have that knack. They get the best out of people.

Julie Last (assistant engineer, *Double Fantasy*): The band [drums, bass, piano, guitars] were spread out in the recording room. Each musician had their "spot" with some baffles between them for a bit of sonic separation. John would sit on a stool in the iso booth and play the song on guitar as the band learned it.

Jack Douglas (producer, *Double Fantasy*): I wanted him in the booth so he could do live vocals and play guitar 'cause he was the greatest rhythm player there was. Good thing I did that because all those live vocals are the only vocals on *Milk and Honey*. I'm sure there are bits and pieces of John's live vocal that made *Double Fantasy*, as well. They just felt so good that I had to use them.

Julie Last (assistant engineer, *Double Fantasy*): Then, when it felt good, we would lay it down. John was in a separate isolation booth where he sang and played guitar. Many of the live vocal takes were wonderful, spontaneous and heartfelt.

Earl Slick (guitar, *Double Fantasy*): John was in a booth, but you could see him. It was so friggin' small, but it was almost like he was in the middle of the room but behind glass. John was in charge of the sessions right from the beginning.

Lee DeCarlo (engineer, *Double Fantasy*): I recently read a quote and it reminded me of John. It said, "If you steal from one person, you're plagiarizing; if you steal from a lot of people, it's research." (laughs) John would actually name who he was ripping off in a particular song (laughs). He was very into Christopher Cross. He thought he was wonderful. John was into a very sailing mood in that time of his life. He had just sailed to Bermuda. I'm not sure what the song was, but he went, "I had this idea from listening to 'Sailing' by Christopher Cross." But he'd also rip himself off. He'd go, "This is from 'I Feel Fine.'"

Andy Newmark (drummer, *Double Fantasy*): When we recorded the basic tracks, John would play and sing live. He'd often go into the control room for a while, just to hear and correct all of our parts, while we kept playing the song. Once he cleaned up all the parts we were playing, he'd come back out into the big room with us and then we'd record. All the tracks on *Double Fantasy* were early takes. By the time we were ready to go for an actual take, he would only play that song six or seven times. The pressure was on us to get a take ASAP. He didn't like playing a song too many times. I believe a lot of his live vocals were used on the record. He was singing for real when we tracked, not singing just a guide vocal. He was always going for a performance, instrumentally and vocally. John is a really good singer. He always sounds exactly like John Lennon.

Earl Slick (guitar, *Double Fantasy*): Sometimes he'd play us a song on guitar and we'd all jump in and play around. It was like a band thing, as you played through the song he would say, "Hey Slickie, can you try this direction?" and "Hughie, can you do this?" Sometimes he'd go, "I'm not really sure what I wanna do with the guitars in this, why don't you guys come up with something?"

Julie Last (assistant engineer, *Double Fantasy*): John was open to discovery and letting things evolve, but the arrangements had been pretty well worked out ahead of time, based, I think, on John's demos. Jack and John and the band had a good sense of how to work with the outline of the arrangements and bring those songs to life.

George Small (keyboards, *Double Fantasy*): If a song came out of the box and it was what John wanted, there wasn't too much direction needed. He really liked to work quickly. A good example was the "Instant Karma" session, which was done in one day. That's an extreme example. He really liked to get it done while it was warm, so to speak. But that's not to say if the band wasn't on to what he was thinking or visualizing he wouldn't take the time to go over it, even musician by musician. Everybody knew what kind of stamp you could put on it. You would sense what the song needed. That's the mind-set of a session player.

Lee DeCarlo (engineer, *Double Fantasy*): I was known for working fast and that's probably one of the reasons I got to work on the record. I knew shortcuts to get the sound I wanted and what the client wanted quickly. I like working fast and so did John.

Jack Douglas (producer, *Double Fantasy*): If it was taking more than three or four takes, he would get really antsy and lose interest quickly, but I knew that from being around him before. You had to stay on top of the players a lot to make sure they understood that.

Andy Newmark (drummer, *Double Fantasy*): He didn't want to play these songs more than five or six times once we were really on the verge of getting one. Therefore, everyone had to play really simple and consistent in order to get a good take quickly, knowing that John wanted to get it within the hour, not five hours. If a player started to stretch out, he would risk blowing the take. Everyone had to stay right inside their parts. John would often say to me, "Keep it simple, Andy, and play like Ringo." That was John's general order to me for the month of tracking. From the first time he told me to play like Ringo, I knew exactly how to approach my playing. Ringo is a total groove player and that is what John likes. Meat and potatoes. That's what they call it in England. Anytime a player went out on a limb and began experimenting, and especially me, the drummer, it could cost the take. If you get a good drum track you can fix other things, but without the drums being right, you cannot proceed. Left to my own devices I am prone to experimenting. John's orders to me kept me right in line with what he wanted from the drums. I prayed daily that Ringo's spirit would inhabit me.

Tony Davilio (arranger, *Double Fantasy*): I remember whenever Andy Newmark thought he made a mistake, he'd say, "Uh-oh, they're gonna get Russ Kunkel." *(Author's note: famed L.A. session drummer who worked with the likes of Bob Dylan, James Taylor, Crosby, Stills and Nash, and Linda Ronstadt.)* He said it in a joking way. He must have said this about fifty times. After a few days of him saying this, John said, "Godammit, Andy, if I wanted Russ Kunkel, I would've gotten him!" But in truth, Andy was the perfect drummer for the sessions.

Jon Smith (assistant engineer, *Double Fantasy*): John instinctively knew what he wanted for each song's arrangement and he knew how to get it. He told people, "Here's what we're going to do at this point in the song. Why don't you play something like this?" He always seemed totally at ease in the studio. One of the first overdubs we did on the whole album was hand claps on "Starting Over." John went out to the mic with Jack and he said he wanted the hand claps to be light claps. Fingers clapping against the palms, not palm on palm. John explained that it would have more personality this way. He always knew what he wanted and it always seemed to work.

Andy Newmark (drummer, *Double Fantasy*): John had a very, very clear idea of the parts that he wanted the band to play. That put us at ease immediately, knowing he was in the driver's seat and able to be so articulate about what he wanted from us. He really knew exactly what he wanted, note for note, if he had to resort to that. I could see all his years of experience in a recording studio coming out now. Although he had not recorded for the five years prior to *Double Fantasy*, John demonstrated that he was still very comfortable and confident in a recording studio. Clearly, he knew his way around in that environment. I was impressed right from the start with his authority, his clarity, and his ability to make decisions fast. He never lost his focus. That was fantastic. We got the leadership, confidence, and authority that we needed. This was unlike many artists who I've worked for who are not leaders in this context, though they may well be amazing talents nonetheless. John really had it all; 1980 is also when John had been straight and sober for several years. I didn't know him before then, but I knew that the John Lennon who was there in front of me in 1980 was incredibly clear, articulate, sober, smart, and totally in the moment. He had no trouble communicating everything he wanted with ease. I admired that very much. I certainly "got it" very quickly when he communicated something to me.

Julie Last (assistant engineer, *Double Fantasy*): It was somewhat intimidating at first working with John. After all, he was a Beatle. But he was very easygoing and funny and so excited to be back in the studio after five years of being a "house husband." His spirit was like a little kid in a candy shop. You just got swept up in his joy at being back to making a record again.

Hugh McCracken (guitar, *Double Fantasy*): We worked at a good pace in the studio. He was a hard worker, but he had fun with everything. We jammed on a lot of fifties and sixties songs. John and I were the same age and we grew up listening to the same music as kids. It became kind of a joke. If I played the beginning to "That'll Be the Day," he couldn't resist going with it (laughs). I would get him, no matter what he was doing, even if there was a whole room of players ready to hear the countoff for the next song.

Tony Levin (bass, *Double Fantasy*): Something I hadn't expected was the goofing around, jamming to Buddy Holly songs. John was thrilled that Hugh seemed to know them all. John would start singing one, Hugh would come in just right, and the rest of us would join in . . . why not? I have to admit, I did not know any of these songs! Then he'd laugh and finish. Hugh would kick back in with another, maybe "Be-Bop-A-Lula." John would jump in and we're playing again. No wonder he'd have to suddenly put a halt to it and get back to recording.

Hugh McCracken (guitar, *Double Fantasy*): When he got down to business, he was very focused. John had a certain pace that he felt comfortable with. Jack also followed that lead. It wasn't a labored process. John would play the songs for us first and perform it by himself. We'd follow the chords on the charts and hone in on our parts. He wouldn't dictate parts to people unless it was part of the song. During the run-throughs he heard everything that was going on. He would tell whoever the player was what he liked and what he didn't like. There wasn't much that he didn't like.

Earl Slick (guitar, *Double Fantasy*): John was the funniest guy I ever worked with in my life as far as working with other musicians. He was funnier than shit. You're looking at a guy who was in the Beatles, a guy who was in the limelight with all the peace movements, but push comes to shove, what you really had was a working-class kid from Liverpool with a damn good sense of humor that loved playing rock and roll music. And he was having a fuckin' ball.

Julie Last (assistant engineer, *Double Fantasy*): In the studio, John was very enthusiastic, silly, but serious, too. When necessary, he would focus intently on working out the music. I remember he also did these funny little countoffs at the beginning of each take.

George Small (keyboards, *Double Fantasy*): His positive energy was infectious. He always had something funny to say. I always felt a sense of respect. He would never get so impatient about something where he would be abusive to anyone in any way.

Earl Slick (guitar, *Double Fantasy*): You walk into a situation like that and you don't know what you're walking into. What's he gonna be like? Is he gonna be tough? Is he gonna be personal or impersonal? Are we gonna go through one of these things where the producer is talking to us and the artist is sittin' in the corner? I've been through that one before. But it was completely the opposite of that, working with John. We walked in there and there was this really cool guy. If I didn't know he was John Lennon and I never heard of the Beatles, I would have still loved the guy and that says a lot. After the first meeting with him you didn't feel that you were in the presence of anyone than another guy in the band. But every once and while I'd think, I'm in the studio with a fuckin' Beatle! What the hell is this? (laughs) Christ almighty, this is cool! With everybody he was very complimentary whenever you locked into something.

Tony Levin (bass, *Double Fantasy*): One knew this would be a special recording. But there were surprises for me, too. I was surprised at what a good producer John was. He thoroughly knew what he wanted. He was remarkably adept at pulling it together and was very specific. He had the ability to hear what was going on. If he heard something completely new to him and different than what he had in mind he could still jump on it and utilize it for the song. He would goof around jamming, or making jokes about the song for a while, but when he decided, "Okay, enough fooling around, let's do it," a switch went off in him. He went into work mode and we had to get right into the take. He'd remarkably remind everyone of their parts, suggest drum fills, get the groove going, and more. It would almost become tense, because you *knew* that there would be no second take, this would be it. He didn't bother to see if tape was rolling. "Let's do it," and he did it. It became kind of a studio joke, "Hugh's in the bathroom" and if even he wasn't, John would say, "He can overdub!" He wasn't gonna slow down for anything. You kind of knew that was gonna be the take. But it was no real tension, just excitement.

Andy Newmark (drummer, *Double Fantasy*): John's vibe was 110 percent upbeat, happy, optimistic, and positive in the studio. He loved every minute of it. Clearly he was having a really good time. It was so apparent to anyone there. He loved being straight, loved Yoko, and was madly in love with his little boy, Sean, who was there at the studio every day after nursery school.

Julie Last (assistant engineer, *Double Fantasy*): I remember one time Sean came to the studio and he went out and started talking into a microphone. Quick thinking, Jack had me plug in a harmonizer on the mic. This is a piece of gear that changes the pitch of things and we set it about four octaves down so that everything Sean said sounded like a huge old man. Then we set it way higher so whatever he said sounded like a chipmunk. Oh, he had so much fun with that! Really got into it. We all laughed like crazy.

Andy Newmark (drummer, *Double Fantasy*): John and Yoko were always hugging and kissing each other. He was in such a good mood all the time. If we weren't playing, he would always be talking away to whoever was around. Once John had his cup of Brazilian coffee—which he said to me was his only remaining drug—that coffee put him right into the groove, big-time. I tried a bit and almost had a heart attack. Man, that stuff was like rocket fuel. He was used to it, though. He kept a bag of Brazilian coffee beans, a grinder, and a coffeemaker in the back room behind the control room. Every couple of hours he would stop and say, "Man, I need another hit of that coffee" and get up and go in the back room and prepare himself some. I'm not surprised at how spontaneous and chatty and sociable he was with everyone all the time. He was grooving like a big dog on that Brazilian coffee. I have to say, I am so glad I met him at this great time in his life.

Julie Last (assistant engineer, *Double Fantasy*): I remember John's working methods in the studio being somewhat relaxed, but everyone knew what a privilege it was to be there. It seemed that everyone was sharing the best of their talent and energy. We recorded something like twenty-five songs. Perhaps a song, maybe two a day?

George Small (keyboards, *Double Fantasy*): There was no slack time on the record except when the sushi arrived at the studio.

Stan Vincent (Jack Douglas's business partner): Every day they'd order these two huge sushi platters. It was the most colorful sushi display you'd ever seen. One day we were in the studio, and the rhythm section was working hard, trying to get a take. John was in the control room and gets on the talkback and says to the entire band, "Gentlemen, the dead fish has arrived." (laughs)

Lee DeCarlo (engineer, *Double Fantasy*): This went on for two weeks straight. Finally, I couldn't eat sushi anymore, so I ordered a burger and ate it in the maintenance shop. Some of the guys in the band found out about it and days later we were eating pizza and

burgers in there. The next couple of days later John and Yoko were the only ones out there eating sushi. We were all in the maintenance shop eating hamburgers. John walked in and said, "What the hell are you doin'?" (laughs) "We're eating burgers, you want one?" And he said, "I haven't had a burger for a long time. Yeah, okay, I'll have one." (laughs)

Lee DeCarlo (engineer, *Double Fantasy*): John had a little lounge area next to the studio. I went in there one day and I was smoking a cigarette and talking to him. There was a great big plate in the lounge. I said, "Is that an ashtray?" And he said, "Yeah." So I put my cigarette out and I said, "Wow, that looks old." And he said, "Yeah, it used to belong to a pharaoh." It was a fruit plate from 3000 B.C. (laughs), and I was using it as an ashtray.

George Small (keyboards, *Double Fantasy*): He was extremely motivated during the sessions. There was never a day where he was laid-back. He always had that combustible energy. John and Yoko had a deadline and wanted to get the record done in time for the Christmas market.

Julie Last (assistant engineer, *Double Fantasy*): The tracks that were chosen for *Double Fantasy* were fleshed out and polished with final lead vocals and additional parts like backing vocals, horns, and solos. The rest of the tracks were set aside to be used for the next album, which became *Milk and Honey*.

Lee DeCarlo (engineer, *Double Fantasy*): He overrecorded for *Double Fantasy*. If there was a second album and he hadn't been murdered, I doubt that any of his songs that wound up on *Milk and Honey* would have made it.

Julie Last (assistant engineer, *Double Fantasy*): It was just as the team was reassembling to begin sessions for *Milk and Honey* that John was tragically shot. John's original live vocals were the only vocal tracks that existed for those songs and so that's what you hear on that record.

Earl Slick (guitar, *Double Fantasy*): I'm really fond of the *Milk and Honey* material, as well. "Nobody Told Me" is one of my favorite songs of all time, let alone Lennon songs. That song was cut at the beginning of the sessions. We were finished with the sessions and I was ready to go back to L.A. where I was living. I got a phone call to come back for one more day at the studio 'cause there were a few more bits John wanted to do. One of them was the "Stepping Out" solo. We stood in the studio facing each other and we did that solo together. The stuff that stands out guitar-wise during the sessions is "I'm Losing You," "Cleanup Time," "Nobody Told Me," and "I'm Stepping Out." We finished *Double Fantasy* and it came out before John was assassinated. We had all these other tracks left. The last conversation I had with John face-to-face was that we were gonna come back into the studio after the first of the year to overdub and finish off the rest of these other tracks for an album that would be put out later on. That included songs like "Nobody Told Me" and "I Don't Wanna Face It," which is a very spooky song.

Hugh McCracken (guitar, *Double Fantasy*): At first, John seemed very insecure about how his audience was gonna like his new music. As the recording progressed, he clearly became more excited and confident.

Jack Douglas (producer, *Double Fantasy*): John and I had a good, trusting relationship and I also had that same relationship with

Yoko. She also trusted me. She knew that I respected her work and that I was a trustworthy person.

Andy Newmark (drummer, *Double Fantasy*): My recollection is that Jack did the most beautiful thing that a producer can do, which was lay way back and stay out of John's way. That's a big plus with any producer and the smart ones know when to do it. John made all the musical decisions. He had a very clear vision for all of that. Jack was very supportive, always keeping an eye on everyone and everything going on, and was someone for John to bounce stuff off of and get an opinion from.

Jack Douglas (producer, *Double Fantasy*): I knew instinctually how to make it work in the studio. My general philosophy about making records is sometimes you need to go in and write with the artist, like I did with Aerosmith. In other situations you facilitate, from doing the budget to making sure the studio is booked to hiring all the musicians. Other times you just have to gently guide the thing along. When you have a talent like John Lennon, do you need to get in his way? No. You just need to let it happen.

Lee DeCarlo (engineer, *Double Fantasy*): Jack is a brilliant producer. John knew what he wanted and Jack helped him facilitate ideas. He was diplomatic. For example, if John had a nugget of an idea, Jack would go away for a day or two and he'd come back and say, "Remember that idea you had? Why don't we try this?" Also, if there was ever a disagreement, Jack was the tiebreaker.

Andy Newmark (drummer, *Double Fantasy*): It's important for an artist to have someone on board whose opinions they trust. John would ask Jack, "Do you think we should do this or do you like the other way we did it?" Jack would go, "You know, I think the other way was better." John trusted his judgment and would go with Jack's instinct. There's a place for what I would call a laid-back kind of producer. An important place. A laid-back personality who maintains an overview of the big picture is a valuable asset in these situations. Jack was supercool and wasn't trying to prove anything to anyone, like, "Hey, I'm a record producer, watch this!" He was cool enough to let John do his thing and yet he was always there when John needed him. Jack always seemed to be able to be objective about things. He was a very stabilizing, calming force. I liked Jack a lot. I thought the chemistry between John and Jack was really good. They were a very good team together.

Tony Davilio (arranger, *Double Fantasy*): Jack was a sounding board. He would make comments or suggestions, but he would follow John's lead. He was concerned with getting the best sounds, making sure the instruments sounded right, making sure there was no distortion and getting the best takes.

Stan Vincent (Jack Douglas's business partner): Jack's a multitalented guy. He's a master in the studio. He's a musician and got his engineering chops while working at the Record Plant. He knew how to get the right sounds and had the knack to know what would work for a song. Jack is fearless. He was open to trying a lot of ideas.

George Small (keyboards, *Double Fantasy*): Jack had the same kind of surprising energy that John had. He would put effect boxes on the guitars and keyboards and sometimes wouldn't care what the logic may be. Sometimes he'd face the knobs the wrong way, just to see what that approach would get in terms of sounds. He was definitely experimental with sounds. He got along great with John. The chemistry in the room was always warm and cordial.

Jack Douglas (producer, *Double Fantasy*): Well into producing the album, I once asked John, "I meant to ask you, why am I doing this record with you?" He said, "Because you have good antenna and that works for me because you always can read me" and that's pretty cool, because I always felt that was one of my strong points. It was very important to him to be able to easily communicate with his producer. And because he was so without ego when he was working, he would take direction. If I told John, "For this vocal, I need you to stand on your head," he'd say, "If you think that's better, I'll do it." John wanted a really tight, thick, and refined New York pop sound. Not terribly different from his past records, but not a raw sound. What was important to him was that he was turning forty and he wanted a mature-sounding record. Lee DeCarlo was the main engineer on the record. He's a supercompetent engineer who got a great sound. He also brought character and I knew that John would really like the guy. The most important thing about how I staffed everything—the players, the engineers—was to make John feel comfortable with the characters.

James Ball (assistant mix engineer, *Double Fantasy*): At the time, Lee DeCarlo was the best engineer in the country. He had great ears and could really capture the clarity of the instruments. He could really dial it in. *Double Fantasy* had that warm, natural sound that Steely Dan might aspire to. The magic of that record is the way it would wrap itself around you. You can put that up against any record today and go, "Wow, that's a great-sounding record." For me, you can compare that record's full-bodied sound to other enduring classic albums like *Damn the Torpedoes* by Tom Petty and the Heartbreakers and *Aja* by Steely Dan.

Lee DeCarlo (engineer, *Double Fantasy*): I'm very proud of the way the album sounds. When you're doing it right, the sound of the record should have a certain characteristic. This particular album had probably the best air of any album I've ever heard. When you listen to the album you can hear it breathe in and out. The way you accomplish that is getting the sonics of the drums and bass to work together so you have what we call a "pulse." Hughie knew when not to play better than anybody in the whole world and he always has. That adds a dimension to the way a song is breathing. John had a plan of the characteristics of his next three, four, five albums. He was gonna build a studio. He was excited by new technology. He didn't realize how far we'd come with synthesizers. He thought it was great and wanted to build a studio with just keyboards sticking out of the walls all over the place.

Tony Davilio (arranger, *Double Fantasy*): When John was recording, Yoko would usually be sitting in the console listening. Sometimes she'd sit there and knit. But she was in and out a lot because she was the business half.

Andy Newmark (drummer, *Double Fantasy*): I recall that Yoko always sat in the control room when John was doing his songs. Just sitting quietly, reading, just being there, being supportive.

Earl Slick (guitar, *Double Fantasy*): She'd be in the control room and there'd be times that she would be putting in some input that wasn't all welcomed (laughs) and it was verbalized by John.

Tony Davilio (arranger, *Double Fantasy*): Yoko might make a critique of something John did and if he didn't agree, he'd say, "Shut up, Mother, and go sell some fucking cows!" (laughs) But he did it tongue in cheek. We'd all laugh and Yoko would laugh, too.

Bob Gruen (photographer and friend): People ask me what kind of woman Yoko is and I say that she's the kind of woman that John Lennon could marry. People tend to forget that side of it.

Earl Slick (guitar, *Double Fantasy*): They had two different kinds of relationships. There was the husband and wife and there was the working team. No one pulled any punches because they were husband and wife. Neither John nor Yoko would be reluctant to express their opinions to each other and sometimes quite bluntly, which was funnier than shit. Nothing ever got heavy. The reaction was no different than it would have been under any other circumstance had you been working with a nonspouse.

Jack Douglas (producer, *Double Fantasy*): There was an effort to make the record be very compatible. What Yoko said the record was supposed to be was a dialogue between the two of them. For it to go off in a really strange direction would not have worked. Yoko gave me plenty of material so I was able to suggest the songs that we should do, so it became more of a song-driven album from both John and Yoko. I made sure to pick songs that wouldn't take her character away because obviously in her vocals she does her Yoko thing.

Tony Davilio (arranger, *Double Fantasy*): Yoko was open to suggestions about her songs in the studio. The band would play and develop the songs. She would sit there, nodding her head. I don't remember her saying too much that she didn't like what was happening with her songs.

Jack Douglas (producer, *Double Fantasy*): When John came in and heard what she did after it was done, it was like, "Yeah!" He'd get really excited.

John Lennon: There's only two artists that I've ever worked with for more than a one-night stand. That's Paul McCartney and Yoko Ono, and I think that's a pretty damned good choice![15]

Jack Douglas (producer, *Double Fantasy*): Getting Yoko's parts done were the biggest challenge. I needed her vocals to be a little more polished than she'd normally do. We didn't have anything that could straighten the pitch, so it meant that I really had to work her hard. She really liked it when it was all done. But I don't think she ever understood the amount of work it took after she would do a part to put it all together. It would take away some amount of confidence on her part. I'd prefer to say, "That was great, can you give me another one?"

Earl Slick (guitar, *Double Fantasy*): Everybody gave Yoko the lead on her stuff, even though John would interject here and there.

Tony Levin (bass, *Double Fantasy*): John would be the "producer," but stay in the control room and largely let her, as the artist, direct how the song would go.

Tony Davilio (arranger, *Double Fantasy*): John was hands-on with Yoko's songs. He stayed in the control room while the songs got developed. He'd be very encouraging to her. The band gave their all, whether they were working on John or Yoko's songs. They wanted to play as good as they could. There was no favoritism.

Tony Levin (bass, *Double Fantasy*): The process was very different, largely because Yoko wasn't playing the song for us. We'd have charts of the chords and would need to begin by finding what kind of feel and tempo would work for it.

Hugh McCracken (guitar, *Double Fantasy*): Yoko has a very distinct style. It was a lot of fun working on her songs because they were more left of center. John treated everything equal, his songs and her songs. We put as much creative attention and time into working on a John song as we did working on a Yoko song.

Jack Douglas (producer, *Double Fantasy*): I really got a kick out of Yoko's material. I mean, John is in a class all by himself, but Yoko was offering really unique and "new"-sounding material and that was exciting.

Julie Last (assistant engineer, *Double Fantasy*): She was really an equal partner in this record. It was meant to be a dialogue between two lovers. This is why it was sequenced to alternate between her tracks and his.

Andy Newmark (drummer, *Double Fantasy*): When we would do Yoko's songs John would take over and direct Yoko's tracks from the control room. He wasn't playing an instrument on her tunes. He would go sit behind the board and she'd come out to the big room and sing with us.

Yoko Ono: John was extremely inspired during the sessions. I thought John would just do his thing and mine would be, "Okay, let's just finish Yoko's." (laughs) That's how it was in the old days and I thought it was gonna be like that and that's what I was used to. It didn't matter to me so much. I could do with it. But what surprised me is John was so supportive of my stuff. That was really surprising.

John Lennon: To work with your best friend is a joy and I don't intend to stop it. If we hadn't had the success we'd had with this record, I would have been quite happy because I know I can live without it. . . . My best friend is my wife. Who could ask for anything more? I'd [just as] soon do something else together than not work together. We feel that this is the start now, you see, *Double Fantasy* is the first album. I know we worked together before. We even made albums together before, but we feel like this is the first album. I feel like nothing happened before today.[16]

Jon Smith (assistant engineer, *Double Fantasy*): When Yoko was cutting songs, John was usually at the console encouraging her. He was somewhat hands-off as I recall, but perfectly happy to put in his ten cents' worth anytime he felt he had something to say. Sometimes Yoko accepted his comments, other times she wouldn't and we'd move on.

Andy Newmark (drummer, *Double Fantasy*): John would direct us from the control room, just like he would on his own songs. He'd say, "Hughie, do that; Earl, do this; Tony, I love that, keep doing it. Hey drummer, don't do that, play like Ringo." He would run the session from the control room. Yoko was pretty laid-back and let John and Jack run the show. She trusted the people around her to do a good job. We did.

George Small (keyboards, *Double Fantasy*): Yoko's songs were challenging in some ways. There's more of an avant-garde leaning on Yoko's songs. Her material is very minimalistic harmonically so what you had to do was think more texturally when you were playing on her songs.

Andy Newmark (drummer, *Double Fantasy*): We cut really good tracks for Yoko. I never knew much about her music before these sessions. It felt honest to me . . . Yoko and us. You know, that's all I really care about and hope for in music. That one word, "honesty," is a big deal to me. If you have that going for you, you have a lot.

George Small (keyboards, *Double Fantasy*): Yoko's recent success with her number one dance club hits, "Walking on Thin Ice" and "No, No, No," show she's finally receiving the credit that John always felt she deserved. She was really ahead of her time and just had a vision and didn't compromise.

Julie Last (assistant engineer, *Double Fantasy*): When it was time to do her vocals we built a little room for her on one side of the studio that was made of sound baffles. When she sang, she went in there, turned down the lights, and we couldn't see her at all. I think there may have been a mattress in there, too, but I might be imagining that. In any case, it was a little bit unusual. John would guide her a little and sometimes he was encouraging and sometimes brutal. Frankly, I didn't resonate with her contribution at the time. John's material and his voice was so much easier to connect with. But her tracks undeniably had great grooves and a very cool vibe.

Jack Douglas (producer, *Double Fantasy*): John changed because of Sean. I sensed that when I ran into him and Sean at that health food restaurant. If he was running on eleven before he was down to about a seven, which is just enough edge.

Jon Smith (assistant engineer, *Double Fantasy*): I recently read the Geoff Emerick book [*Here, There and Everywhere: My Life Recording the Music of the Beatles*]. The whole scene through the book is how angry and unhappy John was. I didn't sense this at all during *Double Fantasy*. He was so happy. He and Yoko were together and they seemed totally at ease with each other. They had this dynamic that any married couple has, where nothing is totally peaceful but you could see that they loved each other very much. There was a mutual respect and admiration. It was fun to watch them interact.

Jack Douglas (producer, *Double Fantasy*): John was the ultimate guy to produce because he was such a true professional. He always left his ego outside the door when he came into work. He was a great rhythm player. He could not play lead to save his life. Very small hands, so he had no reach at all. But man, rhythm. . . . He just had the most amazing feel and rhythm.

Andy Newmark (drummer, *Double Fantasy*): John was primarily a songwriter, more so than a player. However, the parts that he would play on piano or guitar were very connected to the feeling of the track and you really wouldn't want to record a song of his without him playing on it.

Tony Levin (bass, *Double Fantasy*): John had a slightly raunchy approach to playing the parts, but then so do I. I don't remember him making any mistakes.

Hugh McCracken (guitar, *Double Fantasy*): He had an overall gift where whatever he did turned out special. He was a gifted soul. He wasn't a schooled player. Listen to "Get Back," his guitar part is simple and effective. That's what he did best.

Julie Last (assistant engineer, *Double Fantasy*): John's abilities as a guitarist and piano player were very natural. It was neither flashy nor overly simple and it was always unique and interesting.

Andy Newmark (drummer, *Double Fantasy*): He played really simple rhythm guitar and piano, but it was always very in the groove. A lot of songwriters write great songs, but their time is often faulty and tracking gets difficult, as their playing is often speeding up or slowing down. Not John. His time was excellent and he played consistently. He played parts that were full of feeling and you really got that core vibe from him. If he wasn't playing on the basic tracks, we would definitely have lacked something important to guide us. When he played and sang, you got the whole picture immediately. You wouldn't be wondering how to approach the song at all. All I had to do was accompany John in the simplest, most humble way. I would never draw attention to the drums. I stayed invisible as much as possible. I just kept out of his way and gave him a good beat and played right inside of his vocal. You just had to be receptive and open to his vibe and everything would just happen by itself. He was a very evolved and complete musical force.

Tony Davilio (arranger, *Double Fantasy*): John said to me, "I always considered myself a primitive artist." It was all instinct and feel with him. I know he was frustrated because he wasn't a better guitar player. But on his songs his playing was dead-on.

George Small (keyboards, *Double Fantasy*): He was one of a kind. John wasn't a trained musician, but he had such a primitive and raw natural talent. The totality of what John was—his songwriting, his voice, the way he played the guitar, even the way he played keyboards, and the unity of that presence when the energy would come on—would just drive you.

Earl Slick (guitar, *Double Fantasy*): You didn't know who played what on a Beatles record. A George Harrison slide solo is extremely obvious, but not other things. But playing with John, I was surprised at how good a guitar player he was. He was extremely underrated. He had killer feel. When he picked that guitar up, he made it talk. I've never been a fan of technical guitar playing. I don't know what the fuck I'm doin'. I pick up a guitar and whatever comes out comes out. John was that type of player. I find the guys that have a real style are mostly the guys who play from a gut feel. You're not a studied guitar player, but you're communicating emotions through your guitar so your personality is coming out on the instrument. And John was like that.

Lee DeCarlo (engineer, *Double Fantasy*): He had a great three-finger style of playing piano that was really cool and his inversions were very different than what a schooled piano player would play. The very first day that we recorded "Starting Over" he sat down and played "Money," his inversions on that were so strange that it was masterful.

George Small (keyboards, *Double Fantasy*): He would show me how he wanted to voice certain chords on the piano and they'd sometimes be ways that I wasn't used to. Just the way he would play some of these songs and show me these chord voicings came from a guitar player's sensibility. "Watching the Wheels" and "Cleanup Time" were the two songs I remember he also played piano on.

Tony Davilio (arranger, *Double Fantasy*): Before he would sing a lead vocal, John would get a back massage in the little room across the hall from the studio. He said it loosened his vocal cords and he could sing better afterwards.

Lee DeCarlo (engineer, *Double Fantasy*): When laying down a lead vocal, John would change the lyrics as we went along from take to take and they would be cooler (laughs).

Jack Douglas (producer, *Double Fantasy*): I didn't really have to push him when he sang, I just had to direct him. He would come in and do his vocals. I'd record five tracks of lead vocals. I'd tell him to take a few hours off. He'd go into his little room and play piano or do yoga or meditate or get a massage. So I'd take the best parts of those vocal takes and assemble a master. Then John would come in and listen back. Then he'd double that, which he did like no one else in the world could do. He was the perfect doubler.

Julie Last (assistant engineer, *Double Fantasy*): It was a sound he liked on his voice and he was very good at matching his original phrasing. Not too perfect, but close enough to give the lead vocal a "vibe."

Lee DeCarlo (engineer, *Double Fantasy*): He'd double his voice without listening to the original voice in his headphones; he remembered it. Then he'd put that "Mojo filter" effect that he loved, that Elvis kind of delay on his voice. He didn't want to hear himself without that sound on his voice. He used to make fun of his voice, but he knew that he was good. So he'd add that delay to his second vocal and bury his second vocal. This way the delay on his voice is not coming from the voice that you hear, but it's coming from the voice that he used to double with.

Jack Douglas (producer, *Double Fantasy*): He double-tracked because he hated the sound of his voice. And I used to tell him, "John, you don't have to double." These demos from Bermuda were recorded on a Panasonic boom box, it was just acoustic guitar or, in one case, piano on "Real Love" and him and Fred Seaman banging on pots and pans. He actually took the time to play those from one Panasonic to another one and double his vocal because he couldn't bear that I would hear these things with a single vocal.

Julie Last (assistant engineer, *Double Fantasy*): John was very quick with vocals. It wasn't that he didn't care, but rather, it just flowed so naturally from him that every take seemed special.

Jack Douglas (producer, *Double Fantasy*): I remember that "Beautiful Boy" took a little bit longer because of the chorus. Then he would double-track his vocals.

Jon Smith (assistant engineer, *Double Fantasy*): One day, early in the project, as I was setting up the studio, John and Yoko arrived early. Jack and Lee [DeCarlo] hadn't arrived yet and John had an idea for a vocal part, a harmony part that he wanted to record. I loaded the multitrack tape and cued it up, but when we looked at the track sheet, there were no open tracks to put his part on. John said not to worry, there was an old trick they used to do on Beatle records. They would do an overdub on a track that already had something recorded on it, without erasing what was already there, by disconnecting the erase head from that track. The trick of it is to get the new recording at the right level so it's balanced correctly with what's already there, and we'd only get one shot at it so we'd have to get it right the first time. He told me he had faith in me and that he'd take full responsibility when Jack and Lee came. We decided to go right onto the lead vocal track that John had sung when cutting the song. He went out to the studio. We practiced it a few times to get the level right and then recorded it. When we played it back, it sounded great, and when Jack and Lee got there, we played it for them and they loved it.

Jack Douglas (producer, *Double Fantasy*): I remember a major moment during the sessions. John goes out and doubled his vocal on "Watching the Wheels" and came back in and listened to the finished track. He said to Yoko, "Mother, I think we're doing something here. You can let the press know that the record is happening." I think there was a collective sigh of relief from everyone.

Eric Troyer (background vocals, *Double Fantasy*): Jack Douglas brought me onto the sessions. Jack had really pumped him up about me and John was very agreeable to have me come in and sing. Working with John was the high point of my musical life. I showed up for the backing vocal session for "Starting Over" and they'd already started layering parts before I got there. So they said, "Why don't you wait until we start 'Woman' tomorrow?" So then I hung out and ate sushi with Yoko, who was very nice. John was really friendly. I'd been a little bit apprehensive about doing the session. See, Jack had worked with John on a Yoko solo album and it was during the time when John was real caustic and edgy and he was drinking a lot, hanging out with Harry Nilsson. But he was much mellower now. When I talked to him, he said, "I'm totally enjoying being back in the studio. It's totally different for me this time. It's fun. It's not hard work." He was always one to be quick in the studio. He would rush in and get things done and he didn't really want to deal with the details. He just wanted it to sound good. I think he was calmer and he was letting Jack and Lee DeCarlo tweak the sound, which made *Double Fantasy* sound much better.

Tony Davilio (arranger, *Double Fantasy*): One day in the control room John turned to me and said, "Tony, do you want to go to Japan?" I said, "Why?" He said, "There's a synthesizer player over there that I want to use, but we don't know what to tell him to play. You could be the go-between and write down things for him to play." I told him I didn't have my passport and he said, "Well, go get your passport!" I called my wife, Terri, and she worked on getting me a passport. A few days later they told me the Japan trip was off.

Tony Davilio (arranger, *Double Fantasy*): We did a horn session on a Friday night and the session went until three in the morning. That following Monday when I got into the studio, we were in the control room and I heard Jack say to John, "John, how much do you think the horn players cost for that session the other night?" And John looked at him befuddled and said, "A million dollars?" (laughs) Jack was like, "No, seventeen thousand dollars."

Lee DeCarlo (engineer, *Double Fantasy*): John paid this huge bill and came into the studio and told me to erase all of the horns. He stood there and watched me hit record and he turned and looked at the machine to make sure that I was erasing the tracks. That's how pissed he was. I pretended to do it, but erased empty tracks. I figured he might change his mind.

Tony Davilio (arranger, *Double Fantasy*): I wrote out horn parts for a bunch of songs, "Starting Over," "I'm Losing You," "Cleanup Time," and "Yes, I'm Your Angel," but none made the final mix except for "Yes, I'm Your Angel." Also, there's horns on "Cleanup Time."

Tony Davilio (arranger, *Double Fantasy*): We were doing hand claps on a song. John came out and started shadow boxing and swinging his arms. He was like, "Come on, Tony, show me what ya got!" So I went into a boxer's stance and John's jumping around, real animated. We were kind of throwing punches around, but not hitting each other. He was a playful guy. We started laughing and I turned around and he slapped me in the back of the head and ran into the control room (laughs).

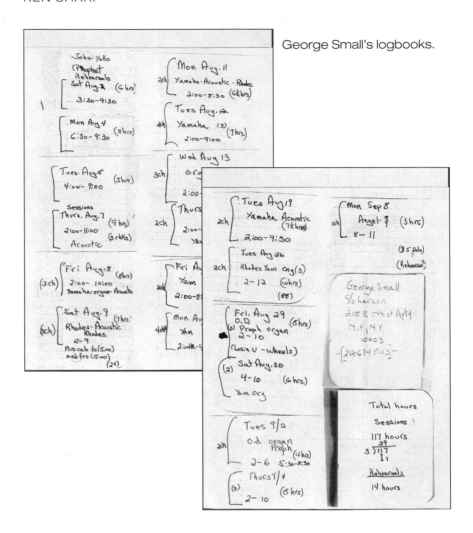

George Small's logbooks.

Stan Vincent (Jack Douglas's business partner): John's birthday was coming up and I said to myself, What the heck do you get John Lennon for his birthday? There was a place out in Montauk called the Rumrunner, which had all this wild and unique stuff. I walked into the store, looked on the wall, and there was half of a crash cymbal, the kind used in marching bands. Stamped on the cymbal in bold letters it said, "Status cymbal" and I just cracked up. I didn't care what it cost, I bought it. I walked into the studio the next week and said, "John, I have something you really need for your birthday." And he gave me a really puzzled look and said, "What's that?" And I said, "A status cymbal." I handed it to him, he opened it up and was hysterical. He took it and nailed it to the wall in the control room at the Hit Factory.

Stan Vincent (Jack Douglas's business partner): John was the most amenable guy you'd ever want to meet. I remember this guy delivered coffee to the studio. John needed to do a vocal and people were saying, "Where's John? Go get John!" and I went out into the waiting room area and there he was, having an intense conversation with the delivery boy who was carrying this white box with all this coffee and Danishes (laughs). That just showed me the warmth of this guy.

Earl Slick (guitar, *Double Fantasy*): At the end of a session we would often sit around and listen back to some of the tracks for reference. John would sit there and tell stories and a lot of it was funny. He loved to talk.

George Small (keyboards, *Double Fantasy*): John's mind was just jumpin' all the time. He'd tell stories that would make you double over laughing or some Beatle fact you never knew about. He liked to tell stories and he was great at it. No question he was the star of the show and deservedly so.

Earl Slick (guitar, *Double Fantasy*): He loved being center stage all of the time and it was fuckin' great. Sometimes we'd prompt him on Beatle stories and he would talk about it. You had to catch him in the right mood. It wasn't gonna happen every time. But every once in a while you'd prompt him and that's how you would get him to sing Beatle songs. You'd be standing in the studio and there'd be a break and one of us would start playing something and sometimes he would jump right in and sometimes he wouldn't. It would just depend on which way the wind was blowin'.

John Lennon self-portrait, 1980.

Jack Douglas (producer, *Double Fantasy*): After the sessions, John never left immediately; he'd always sit in the control room and usually took a little grass. He had this old opium pipe, it was probably five hundred years old, and he'd say to me, "Is it all over?" 'Cause he would never do anything if we were working. And I'd say, "It's over, John." And he'd sit back and put his feet up on the console and he'd load up the pipe and sit back and light up.

Jon Smith (assistant engineer, *Double Fantasy*): He did two drawings on legal pads while we were doing the sessions. One of them was a naked guy on a beach squatting down taking a dump. The other one was a self-portrait of just his face and underneath he wrote "Yes Dear." They were both done with black grease pencil. When Yoko would say something that annoyed him, he would hold it up and say, "Yes, dear." (laughs) At the end of the project when they were cleaning out the studio, I found the two drawings in the garbage. I said, "What are you crazy, you're throwing these away?!" So I grabbed both of the drawings. One of the guys who worked there at the studio with me said, "I want one, too," so he took the one of the guy on the beach and I took the self-portrait.

A Lost Song

In the course of recording the *Double Fantasy* album, John and Jack Douglas collaborated on a song that would ultimately never see the light of day.

Jack Douglas (producer, *Double Fantasy*): John had a song that we never recorded and I would have been listed as the co-writer. It was called "Street of Dreams." After we left the studio we used to go to Rousseau of London, which was the only place in New York where you could get a full English breakfast at two in the morning. We'd walk in and they'd usher us to the back and we'd have a full English breakfast—grilled bread, greasy eggs, the whole bit. After we ate, we'd jump in the limo. We'd pass Carnegie Hall and I said to John, "You know what they call this?" And he said, "What?" And I said, "The street of dreams." At the turn of the century all of the great musicians, opera singers, and the maestros were all on the street. People from all over the world came here to break into various parts of the industry. He said, "I like that." The next day he said, "Come meet me at the studio," and we sat at the piano. We started working on a chorus to an existing verse of his. He said, "That's a verse I've had since the Beatle days." It was one he could never find a chorus for since the mid-sixties. It was very cool. All I remember is the chorus went, "Here on the street of dreams . . ." That was the opening line. The verse had a real Beatle-y feel. We made a little recording of it on the spot. Somewhere there's a cassette of it. I've never heard it again.

Jon Smith (assistant engineer, *Double Fantasy*): John had a business meeting the night before on Fifty-seventh Street. He told us when they walked out of the building it was nighttime and the concrete on Fifty-seventh Street had little pieces of glass embedded in it. He told us as he walked the lights would shine on these things and it would sparkle in a very magical way. It inspired him so much that he'd written a song called "Street of Dreams." He played it for us and it was beautiful and he never recorded it as far as I know. I always wish we could have recorded it because I remember it being lovely. Sometimes, years later, when I'd be falling asleep, I could almost remember what it sounded like.

The Cheap Trick Sessions

Skillfully marrying hard rock with a distinctly Beatlesque flair, by 1980, Cheap Trick were bonafide rock superstars, riding high on the success of their blockbuster album, *Cheap Trick at Budokan*. On August 12, 1980, Cheap Trick guitarist, Rick Nielsen, and drummer, Bun E. Carlos, walked into the Hit Factory, primed to play a session with one of their musical heroes. They would go on to record versions of "I'm Losing You" and "I'm Moving On."

Jack Douglas (producer, *Double Fantasy*): I remember calling up Ken Adamany [Cheap Trick's manager] first to arrange it, to see if it could be done. I remember Ken giving me the hardest time about the, you know, "Well, will they pay their airfare?" and I'm like, "*Hello*, I'm asking you to come up and have the guys play with John Lennon," you know? So don't worry about that stuff, please. [He's like,] "Well, will we get a piece of the record?" I'm like, "Ken, man, let's get going. Talk to the band and see what they want to do," and they were like, "Of course!" John had no idea who they were. He thinks he might have heard of them, but here was the thing, they were so influenced by the Beatles that it made perfect sense to me. Had we continued along those lines, I would have had Robin

[Zander] in there singing backgrounds with them. I mean, it just would have been an absolutely perfect relationship. I knew that those guys were big fans, just as big a fan as I was of John and it was like two reasons I did it, because I knew it was a perfect marriage for John and I did it 'cause I love the band.

Bun E. Carlos (Cheap Trick): We got a call about a month or two ahead of time from our office with the message, "Bun E., call Jack." I called him and Jack said, "John Lennon is gonna record and I want you to play drums on this song, 'I'm Losing You.'" Then he said, "Don't tell anybody" and I immediately told the other guys in the band. It was all big top secret. The reason it was top secret is CBS was trying to sign Lennon. They had Ringo and they had Paul on the label, they wanted to get all four Beatles signed to CBS and they were battling with Geffen over it. Then about two or three weeks later we heard from Jack, who said, "We're gonna have Rick play guitar, too."

Andy Newmark (drummer, *Double Fantasy*): Jack Douglas brought in Cheap Trick's rhythm section to record several songs.

Jack Douglas (producer, *Double Fantasy*): I felt that it needed the edge that the guys from Cheap Trick would give it.

Rick Nielsen (Cheap Trick): We added a raw edge to the songs, and gave them a sound that harkens back to the Plastic Ono Band.

Andy Newmark (drummer, *Double Fantasy*): They wanted to try some things with another rhythm section. It wasn't because we were having any problems with our rhythm section. It was because Jack produced Cheap Trick and knew them well and thought some of the tunes would sound good with them playing. That's what producers are supposed to do, to think about all the possibilities. I think Jack decided right from the beginning that he would cut some of John's songs with Cheap Trick. It wasn't like we were members of John's band and he was blowing us off to work with other people. We were just hired session people. That's often what producers and artists do. That's the freedom one can have as a solo artist, unlike being in a band. Producers will often record songs with different players until they get something they like.

Jon Smith (assistant engineer, *Double Fantasy*): We did that session on a day off.

Rick Nielsen (Cheap Trick): We finished a Canadian tour on August 11. The following day Bun E. and I went to New York and worked with Lennon.

Bun E. Carlos (Cheap Trick): We flew in that morning from Montreal on our day off before we were leaving to go on tour in Japan. We were excited, but also beat. We'd been on the road for a better part of two or three years.

Rick Nielsen (Cheap Trick): I got a phone call early that morning from my wife that we had a bouncing new baby boy named Daxx. I would have made sure I'd been at home for the birth of our son, but my wife gave me a hall pass knowing it was a John Lennon session. So the day started out terrific and it got even better knowing we were going to be playing with John.

Bun E. Carlos (Cheap Trick): We went walking up the stairs of the Hit Factory and Bob Gruen was outside taking pictures. We get into the elevator and saw this bald guy. We'd seen the footage of John Lennon at the Lew Grade benefit show right before he retired. He did "Slippin' and Slidin'" and "Imagine" and he was backed by the Band of Mother Fuckers (BOMF) and the whole band were bald. I turned to this bald guy and said, "Are you by chance a member of BOMF?" And he said, "I'm Tony Levin, I don't know what you're talking about." So we went into the studio and we were introduced to John and Yoko. When you meet these famous guys they're always shorter than you think. John was smaller than I expected. They introduce us, "This is Bun E. and Rick," and he goes, "Oh, you're the guys from Cheap Trick. They told me your name, but they didn't tell me what band you were in." So he recognized us from being in Cheap Trick, which we thought was cool. John was really friendly. He was Mr. Nice Guy.

Rick Nielsen (Cheap Trick): I had the ultimate ice breaker and told him that I'd had a baby that day. Later in the session we all ended up smoking these Cuban cigars I'd picked up at the airport. We toasted to my wife and our new baby, Daxx, and also to John and Yoko's son, Sean.

Jack Douglas (producer, *Double Fantasy*): Rick and Bun E. were only nervous for a few minutes. But you have to understand it was difficult to be nervous around John because he was the kind of person to put you at ease immediately. That was part of his magic. He was a musician and when he met other musicians he just got right into it. He just spoke that language. He wasn't like, "John Lennon, Beatle." He was a guy who wanted to play and have fun. More than anything, that was what he lived for.

George Small (keyboards, *Double Fantasy*): I walked into the sessions and went, "Where is everybody?" It was a surprise to me. That was an adjustment to make. We'd congealed into a band rather quickly, not that I didn't feel the same with the Cheap Trick guys, too.

Bun E. Carlos (Cheap Trick): We sat in the control room with John and Jack [Douglas] and they played us a cassette demo of "I'm Losing You" with him on acoustic guitar. He'd been down to Bermuda and had two ghetto blasters. He'd sit there and record guitar and vocal on one and then aim it at the other one and lean over and do overdubs like that on the second machine. John said, "We don't have a good version of this, do you guys have any ideas?" When Jack called us he said, "We've got this song and I know you can do this tempo real good. The session guys don't have a feel for it." We were just glad to be there. We knew it would be fun to do. I mean, how often do you get to play with a Beatle? So we listened to the tune a couple of times and mapped it out.

Rick Nielsen (Cheap Trick): John gave us chord charts so we knew roughly how the song went. I thought the song should have a "Cold Turkey" feel with a riff going through it.

Jack Douglas (producer, *Double Fantasy*): I played the demo for them and they went out in the studio and started to jam the tune. "I'm Losing You" was a song that could be jammed. Bun E. fell right into it and John was out there, like digging it. Tony Levin, you know, amazing bass player, got into a groove, and Rick and John collaboratively came up with [imitates "I'm Losing You" riff]. That was a riff that John liked to play. He felt that right away. Rick and John were both playing live together and it was just magic immediately in the room. You could feel it.

Tony Davilio (arranger, *Double Fantasy*): They brought a real raw approach to the songs. It was a different kind of energy.

Julie Last (assistant engineer, *Double Fantasy*): The tracks they played had a wilder feeling and more rock energy than the other material had, not better or worse, just different.

Rick Nielsen (Cheap Trick): We jammed and had fun. I really liked "I'm Losing You." It had that eerie, creepy, haunting melody and a real edge.

Bun E. Carlos (Cheap Trick): The whole band tracked the song live. John played guitar and sang, I played drums, Rick played guitar, Tony Levin played bass, and George Small was on keyboards. Tony had the fretless bass and George on piano. With those two guys and Lennon, the road was paved for us musically. Those guys were all top dogs and it was really a pleasure to do. John was like Chuck Berry, he was the perfect rhythm guitar player. I noticed that when we were playing together and his sound was in my cans [headphones]. I thought, Oh, here we go. I don't even have to do anything except sit and play along. It was the same feeling I got when we opened for Chuck Berry seven years earlier.

We walked through the song a couple of times. Rick came up with the song's main riff and I came up with some drum parts. I asked, "What speed do you want this?" And John said, "Oh, whatever speed you think it should be." They just kind of let me and Rick take the lead on it. We did a few takes and that was it.

Tony Levin (bass, *Double Fantasy*): That session was great fun for me. I'd already done the songs with the other rhythm section and was really enjoying doing heavier rock versions of them. If it had been up to me, I'd have chosen for the whole album to go that way.

George Small (keyboards, *Double Fantasy*): Those guys were so much fun. We were having a blast. Everybody was just soaring. The whole thing was cookin'. Bun E. and Rick played their asses off. Like Andy Newmark, Bun E. was a real pocket drummer. He and Tony Levin just locked into a groove. Rick went insane on the guitar solo on "I'm Losing You." That was cracking everybody up. It was off the hook, he just started spilling out thousands of notes.

Lee DeCarlo (engineer, *Double Fantasy*): On "I'm Losing You," Rick Nielsen played one of the best solos I have ever heard in my life and it was just one note over and over again, just inflected differently. It was very reminiscent of "Helter Skelter."

Rick Nielsen (Cheap Trick): I put in a Chinese counterrhythm to the song in the solo section to give it a different feel because otherwise the song was pretty straight.

Bun E. Carlos (Cheap Trick): Rick did the solo live and then he went and doubled his solo, which is not on the record. It was meant to be doubled so it would be more of a prevailing theme. The guitar part was kind of orchestrated. While Rick was doubling it, I was in the booth with Lennon and he said, "Do you want to smoke a joint?" And I said, "Yeah, sure, no problem!" I remember when Rick was doing lead and John said, "Your guitar work is great. [Eric] Clapton did something like this on 'Cold Turkey,' but he could only do one lick." I think I said, "We're just trying to give it a Plastic Ono Band feel." That's where we were coming from because Cheap Trick were big Plastic Ono Band fans. We did "Cold Turkey" and

"It's So Hard." John was having a good time on that session. We all had a lot of laughs.

Rick Nielsen (Cheap Trick): I told John we wanted him to produce Cheap Trick's first album, but that was in the late seventies and we thought he was retired from music. And John surprised me by saying, "Oh, I would've done it!" I think John really liked us. Unfortunately, we don't think our manager ever asked him.

Jack Douglas (producer, *Double Fantasy*): John dug 'em. I told him George Martin was producing them at that time [*All Shook Up*], which was really funny because I remember having a talk with George, "You got my act and I got yours."

Julie Last (assistant engineer, *Double Fantasy*): Cheap Trick were very influenced by the Beatles. The night they came, they were in heaven to be playing with John. I remember lots of goofing around and camaraderie. A good time was had by all.

Jon Smith (assistant engineer, *Double Fantasy*): They did the takes and I remember Lee [DeCarlo] said to me, "Did you see what Rick does while he's playing?" I said, "No, what does he do?" He has this thing he does while he's playing where he throws his guitar picks. He keeps a bunch of picks taped to his music stand and so he plays a little bit and tosses it and then grabs another one and plays some more. Apparently he was doing it in the studio during takes.

Jack Douglas (producer, *Double Fantasy*): John took notice of Rick's pick throwing and was cracking up about it. He had a bunch of the Rick Nielsen picks in his pocket.

Jon Smith (assistant engineer, *Double Fantasy*): After the session I remember finding a bunch of picks all over the floor.

Bun E. Carlos (Cheap Trick): After Rick was done overdubbing, Lennon asked, "What are you guys doing later? Do you want to stay and do a song after dinner?" I said, "I gotta go back home and pack my bags, we're going to Japan tomorrow." John had a Groucho Marx look with his eyebrows going up, "Oh yeah, I married one of the emperor's daughters, you know?" and then he laughed. That was some of his classic humor.

Bun E. Carlos (Cheap Trick): "I'm Losing You" was supposed to cross-fade into "I'm Moving On" and they were both about the same tempo. Jack said, "Your beat on 'Loser' (*Author's note: a Cheap Trick song*) would work great on 'Moving On.'" So we had the sheet music from Yoko and it just had chords listed and the melody on it. Rick came up with these riffs [imitates guitar riff from "I'm Moving On"]. Rick wrote the riff for that and I tried this drum part. We were messing around with it because there was no arrangement for it. Tony [Levin] was messin' around with this funky bass riff and he said, "Maybe we could do it like this in the first verse?" Yoko was in the vocal booth and John was in the control room with Jack. We're trying to get an arrangement. John gets on the talkback and goes, "Mother dear, perhaps you can do the first verses like Tony and then do the boys' arrangement after the first verse." He called Rick and I "the boys." Yoko turned to John and gave him a look and said, "Fuck you very much, John!" and everybody started laughing.

Rick Nielsen (Cheap Trick): You could tell that John and Yoko had a good rapport in the studio. They worked very well together.

Bun E. Carlos (Cheap Trick): Our version of "I'm Moving On" is a lot barer than the record 'cause it was done live in the studio. Her vocal on it is pretty raw. It's very cool. At the end she went into her gurgle-gargling "Don't Worry Kyoko" vocal thing and everybody playing went, "Oh yeah, we're in Yokoland now." We did a couple of takes with Yoko singing live. Our take wasn't the best take in the world. The drums were a little faltering so the one on the record is probably a little better.

Bun E. Carlos (Cheap Trick): We asked, "Ya got anything to eat around here?" Yoko had this granola stuff for snacks, like something you'd feed squirrels. She said, "Yeah, try some of this stuff." Meanwhile, John was running into this little room to have a slice of pizza for lunch.

Rick Nielsen (Cheap Trick): He was really personable right off the bat. John took me around the studio and showed me the big huge guitar on the wall. He also took me to the storage room and showed me some of his guitars and his mellotron. I told him I had the first mellotron in the United States besides CBS-TV and maybe the Beach Boys. We connected like kids talking about guitars.

Jon Smith (assistant engineer, *Double Fantasy*): John had brought some old guitars in and one of them was his black Rickenbacker guitar from the Beatles days. He showed it to Rick and Bun E. and the amazing part was that it still had Scotch taped onto it the set list from the Beatles' Shea Stadium concert.

Rick Nielsen (Cheap Trick): He let me play his Rickenbacker and that was a thrill.

Bun E. Carlos (Cheap Trick): John said, "This is my 'Day Trip-per' guitar, I had it refinished." And I said, "Oh yeah, 'Day Tripper,' that's number ten in Phoenix this week." He goes, "What do you mean?" I said, "Yeah, we got a live version on an EP [*Found All the Parts*] and our office told me it was number ten in Phoenix this week." He didn't expect that (laughs).

Stan Vincent (Jack Douglas's business partner): John had his Rickenbacker in his hand and said, "You see this? I'm gonna give this guitar to the Smithsonian." I said, "I wouldn't dare do that. You know where that guitar is gonna go?" and I pointed to Sean's picture on the TV in the control room. And he went, "Oh yeah, right!" (laughs)

Jack Douglas (producer, *Double Fantasy*): Rick took pictures of John's Rickenbacker and measured it. Then two weeks after those sessions a package arrived for John at the studio and it's a custom-made white Hamer guitar. Rick was endorsing that company at the time. Everything on the guitar was white. It was the same dimensions of the Rickenbacker; John had small hands so he liked that three-quarter-sized neck. There's one picture of him holding that guitar up in a magazine. He was flipped out by it. It was a John Lennon model 001. It was a one-off. It was all white except for one thing. John paid Rick and Bun E. for the session and he signed the checks. So Rick had a copy of his signature. He made the signature bigger and this guitar was all white, except John's signature was at the bottom of it in red mother-of-pearl. That guitar was just gorgeous.

Rick Nielsen (Cheap Trick): It's now in the Lennon exhibit at the Rock and Roll Hall of Fame.

Bun E. Carlos (Cheap Trick): Rick had a Fender Telecaster with a string-bender. They're real collectible guitars.

Rick Nielsen (Cheap Trick): He saw me messing around with this Fender B-bender guitar and liked my playing. He'd never seen a guitar like that and really liked it.

Bun E Carlos (Cheap Trick): At the end of the day, Rick said, "Take this and mess around with it. Let me loan it to you and I'll just get it back from you later." So he left the guitar with Lennon and he got it back a few years later from Yoko. Before I left the session I got John and Yoko to sign the sheet music, which was a good move. John wrote, "To Bunny, Enjoyed the hop, Love John Lennon" and drew a picture of himself.

Andy Newmark (drummer, *Double Fantasy*): The same process of chemistry that took place between our rhythm section and John and Jack could have happened with Cheap Trick. We were simply lucky because we were the first ones to go into the studio with John and Jack. We got in there for the first two weeks of recording. Then when the Cheap Trick sessions came along, it was probably quite an abrupt change from the way we played, which of course is why one would try other players in the first place. Different players, different feel, different vibe, et cetera. Maybe it was too much of a departure from what we had done for the bulk of the record, which we had already recorded before the Cheap Trick sessions took place. Who knows? Had Cheap Trick started the sessions and been working with John and Jack for two or three weeks and then we guys came in for a day, it would have been just as abrupt of a change. Neither section is better or worse than the other, just different. I have been on both sides of that scenario many times. Sometimes I am replacing some other cats and sometimes others are replacing me. It comes with the job when you are a recording musician. No one takes it personally. I certainly don't. I remember we came back in to work after the Cheap Trick sessions and John said, "The tracks went great, but we want to cut the songs with you guys as well and then we'll pick." That's the way to do it. Cut as much as you can with as many different musicians as you can, and then pick what you like.

Rick Nielsen (Cheap Trick): We made up riffs for both those songs ["I'm Losing You" and "I'm Moving On"] and they were copied.

Bun E. Carlos (Cheap Trick): When the band later recut those songs for the album they didn't clone our version. But they copied Rick's riffs on the songs and they did our arrangement of "Moving On," too. Jack told me, "We cut those songs and had the band play along with it a few times on headphones to try and get the same feel you guys had." When we heard that we started laughing, we thought those guys must wanna kill us (laughs). We were thinking, Boy, if someone asked us to do that, we'd sure put our unhappy faces on.

Jack Douglas (producer, *Double Fantasy*): We played the Cheap Trick track in their headphones and they played along with it, and that's how I recorded it. I don't think Andy ever quite got the feel. Andy has his own feel and you just can't copy Bun E. I kind of wish Cheap Trick played on the entire album. Cheap Trick with Lennon on "I'm Losing You" sounds like a hit record. It was so cool.

Bun E. Carlos (Cheap Trick): After the sessions we went to Japan and did three shows. We flew back home and we flew back to New York to do one more song. That was probably gonna be "Nobody Told Me" or "Grow Old with Me." We got there and they were setting up a mix for that song with the reggae guitar ["Borrowed Time"]. John went, "I don't think I'm gonna cut this last song, we've got more than enough stuff." He said, "Sorry, guys, but thanks for coming." So we went back to the airport and came back home. Jack told Robin [Zander] and Rick that he might want them to come back and do some harmonies, but that didn't happen.

Jon Smith (assistant engineer, *Double Fantasy*): I loved the tracks. I thought they were driving and hard. They achieved a harder sound than the rest of the record, which to some degree was their downfall. They simply didn't fit in with the other songs.

George Small (keyboards, *Double Fantasy*): Even though as curios those are interesting versions of the songs, I guess it just didn't fit the concept of the album.

Rick Nielsen (Cheap Trick): They said our stuff sounded too rough, it wasn't compatible with the rest of the tunes. It sounded different.

Bun E. Carlos (Cheap Trick): Sonically, our versions didn't fit in with the rest of the record. It would have been like an orange in the middle of a batch of apples. People would have went, "What the hell is this?" (laughs) I thought the finished versions were real slick. I thought our versions were cooler.

Lee DeCarlo (engineer, *Double Fantasy*): I thought it was better, and John thought it was better, too, than the tracks that made the record, but it was just too aggressive for the nature of the album.

Bun E. Carlos (Cheap Trick): After the sessions we went over to Japan and word already reached them there that we were working with him. It was like the worst best-kept secret in the world. When we did press in Japan somebody said, "I hear you're working with John Lennon" and we said, "Yeah, we worked with him, but we don't know what's gonna happen."

Jack Douglas (producer, *Double Fantasy*): From my perspective those versions didn't make it because Yoko thought we were giving Cheap Trick a free ride. "Who were they to be playing on this record?"

Stan Vincent (Jack Douglas's business partner): I don't believe

Yoko realized how big Cheap Trick was at the time. They weren't riding on anyone's coattails.

Jack Douglas (producer, *Double Fantasy*): John liked that track so much, but it wasn't worth going up against Yoko for that one. She didn't realize that they were established and in fact were doing a record with George Martin at the time [*All Shook Up*].

Bun E. Carlos: (Cheap Trick): We heard that Yoko thought we were getting publicity on John's back, which struck us at the time as kind of ridiculous because John hadn't had an album out in five years and we had a top five album. We thought that was kind of goofy.

Stan Vincent (Jack Douglas's business partner): Cheap Trick was on Epic Records, which was owned by CBS. Yoko had a false fear that if they played on a track, CBS could take claim of John's album (laughs). The concept alone was ludicrous.

Tony Davilio (arranger, *Double Fantasy*): After Cheap Trick laid down the tracks for those two songs, I remember walking into the control room one day, and John had his feet up and was reading *Rolling Stone*. All of a sudden I heard him say, "Goddammit, son of a bitch! Who let this info out to them? I didn't want the press to know anything about them being up here!" It said Cheap Trick was up at the Hit Factory working on John and Yoko's new album. (*Author's note: The September 18, 1980, issue of* Rolling Stone *features a Random Notes report on Lennon's new album featuring assistance from Cheap Trick.*)

George Small (keyboards, *Double Fantasy*): John took this pen like it was a knife and starting digging a big X across the article. It was very shocking because it was right on the heels of everybody being so up about that session. It was one of the few times that I saw him angry. I think that's why their tracks weren't used on the album.

Jon Smith (assistant engineer, *Double Fantasy*): John said he didn't like the tracks because they sounded too much like "Cold Turkey" and that was the past and he was moving on to a new sound. I think John was at a point in his life where he wasn't feeling the angst that he was when he was doing "Cold Turkey" and it just wasn't what he was looking for.

Yoko Ono: They didn't make it onto the album because John didn't want it. John didn't think it was right for the album. He wanted to do it his way.

Bun E. Carlos (Cheap Trick): The tracks never came out. Then in 1996 or '97 we heard from Yoko that they wanted to use our version of "I'm Losing You" on the Lennon box set. It was neat that it was finally out there. I was proud of it when we did it and glad it still sounded good years later. For many years we told people, "We did this thing with John Lennon and it never came out." You can imagine people thinking it mustn't have been that good if it didn't come out. Yoko asked us if we wanted to do a music video for it with Tony Levin and we did it.

Rick Nielsen (Cheap Trick): For me, playing with John was the ultimate. Nothing can top that experience. John Lennon was the guy, he had everything. He was the real deal and lived up to all my expectations. He's my kind of a guy—eccentric, talented, smart, and he played guitar by feel, like an old Delta bluesman.

Bun E. Carlos (Cheap Trick): Sean Lennon came to a sound check of ours in Philly. Our ride never showed up so we didn't go to sound check. We showed up later and my roadie said, "Sean Lennon is here. He was talking about you guys working with his dad. He said, 'I can't believe my dad was hip enough to be working with a cool band like Cheap Trick.'" (laughs) He had it all backwards. It was us who thought it was kinda neat to work with John. We knew that session was special when we were doing it. It's one of the highlights of my music career.

That's a Wrap

By early September, the basic tracks for the album were completed.

Stan Vincent (Jack Douglas's business partner): We finished with all the basic tracks and everyone was about to go to Mr. Chow's, this very exclusive Chinese restaurant in the city. I'm a guy that likes to stay in the background. They were taking a group shot and I stayed in the control room. Everyone assembled and John kept motioning for me to come into the studio for this shot and I refused. John finally said, "I'm not gonna take this photo unless you're in it!" So I ran into the studio and I'm positioned in the front row. I wouldn't have that photo today if John didn't insist on me being in it.

The Beatles

Ten years since the breakup of the Beatles, during the *Double Fantasy* sessions, Lennon would readily tell stories about the band and occasionally jam on an old Beatles tune.

John Lennon: If anything, I'm arrogant about the Beatles and what happened in the Beatles. That's another good thing about the last five years. It has enabled me to look back at that period without being tense about it. I can see a lot of things more clearly now. Tennessee Williams said he slept through the sixties. Well, I didn't sleep through the seventies, but I certainly had blinders on. Those years just went by. It's good to be wide awake again.[17]

Julie Last (assistant engineer, *Double Fantasy*): In the five years he had been away from recording there had been some major advancements in recording technology. He seems to always have had a visionary curiosity and aptitude for experimenting with sound. So when we would plug in some piece of gear to get a certain effect he would be amazed. And it would sometimes trigger stories about how they did it in the "Beatle days." For example, digital delays had now replaced tape loops. Oh man, when he started reminiscing, everything would *stop*. And we would all be like a bunch of kids sitting at an elder's knee, just hanging on every word.

Andy Newmark (drummer, *Double Fantasy*): He spoke about the Beatles a lot during the sessions. He would always refer to them as the Bs. "Oh man, the Bs did this and the Bs did that." In the ten years that had elapsed since the Bs broke up, I felt he'd done his solo thing, his John Lennon underground protest warrior thing. He'd gotten all of that out of his system. He made all the "out there" music that he wanted to make. He came out of it ten years later and was able to look back on that body of work that the Bs had done, and was really proud of them. That is how it seemed to me. He never spoke about the Beatles in a negative way. Ever. He only said positive, affectionate things about them. It seems by this point, in 1980, he was able to look back at their work and realize how great a band they were. I loved it when I would feel that affection and that pride coming from him about the Beatles. It's the happy ending that we all want to hear about that amazing four-piece band.

Tony Levin (bass, *Double Fantasy*): There was that funny feeling sometimes when he'd first play a new song for us. I'd be just drinking it in—feeling, This is great—then there'd be some little sequence of familiar chords or vocal phrase and my instinctive inner "Uh-oh, too much like the Beatles, I'll have to come up with some line to take it elsewhere" . . . But then, Oh yeah, it's John . . . and he's just being himself.

George Small (keyboards, *Double Fantasy*): One day he came into the studio and he took out the guitar that he played on *The Ed Sullivan Show*. Everybody just went "Whoa!" He played a little bit on it and he turned it over, and even he was flabbergasted a bit by this, the set list was still taped to the back from *The Ed Sullivan Show*.

Lee DeCarlo (engineer, *Double Fantasy*): I remember we were editing something and John was bored so he went out into the studio, grabbed the Fender Telecaster B-bender guitar that Rick Nielsen gave him, plugged it in, and sat on the amp all day playing Beatles songs. It was great, you'd walk by and you'd hear him singing and playing "I Want to Hold Your Hand."

Earl Slick (guitar, *Double Fantasy*): Every once in a while me and Hughie would start playing a Beatles lick and he would chime in and sometimes he wouldn't. I remember we played some of "I Feel Fine" and a number of other Beatles songs where he'd forgotten the chords or forgot the words (laughs). We did "She's a Woman." I was the one who started in on it—it's a McCartney song—and at one point, you hear John saying, "Stop playin' that fuckin' thing." (laughs) I don't know if that made it onto any of the released bootlegs.

Hugh McCracken (guitar, *Double Fantasy*): I remember I started playing a little bit of "She's a Woman" and John started to sing it. On the guitar it sits well in the key of E, but that wasn't the key the song was originally recorded in by the Beatles. He said, "What fuckin' key are you doing it in?" He sang a little bit of it, but said it was too high a key to sing and we stopped.

Jack Douglas (producer, *Double Fantasy*): Whenever we did Beatles stuff, he would always tell us that the original recordings were screwed up and that if he had his druthers he would do it again. We'd all say, "John, it's impossible, there's no way to beat it."

John Lennon: I'm too involved in them artistically. I cannot see them objectively. I cannot listen to them objectively. I'm dissatisfied with every record the Beatles ever fucking made. There ain't one of them I wouldn't remake . . . including all the Beatles records and all my individual ones.[18]

George Small (keyboards, *Double Fantasy*): He was very dissatisfied with the way "Strawberry Fields" came out and I have no idea why. Go figure that out. He talked about wanting to redo that song, this was in addition to the tracks we'd done for *Double Fantasy* and *Milk and Honey*. We were doing a Prophet 5 synthesizer on that record. We were all in the control room and John start talking about "Strawberry Fields." Arbitrarily, it was just turned on. There was no specific program. Then he started playing the mellotron beginning of the song. It had an identical sound on the Prophet 5. When that happened, everybody's jaw just dropped, even John. It was uncanny. It sounded like he started playing the record. That's how exact the sound was and no one had set it up that way.

Tony Davilio (arranger, *Double Fantasy*): I was working in the studio and John comes out with his guitar and goes, "Tony, I want to redo 'Strawberry Fields' for the next album and this is how I wanna do it." And he started playing and singing the whole song to me. He told me he always wanted to redo that song and make it less psychedelic. The version he played me had a chugging, rhythmic feel. It was real powerful. I was blown away (laughs). I'm sitting there and here's John singing one of the greatest Beatles songs to me. It was like my own mini-concert.

Lee DeCarlo (engineer, *Double Fantasy*): He could never stand not hearing something come through the speakers. There always had to be music. So two faders on the console were coming from a local New York radio station. When nothing was going on he'd reach over to the two faders, push them up, and then there'd be music coming out. When we'd get ready to record, we'd pull those two faders down. Once when we were mixing at the Record Plant, we stopped, John brought up the two faders and it was "Strawberry Fields," and he went, "Oh, it's me" and pulled them down right away (laughs).

George Small (keyboards, *Double Fantasy*): I told John that I had an arrangement for "Penny Lane." Then I played the song on piano for John and Yoko. When I finished playing it for them, over the talkback mike, John said, "The author approves." That made me probably faint for a second. Just the fact that I had the balls to do that kind of blows my mind today.

Lee DeCarlo (engineer, *Double Fantasy*): I asked him one day, "John, what broke up the Beatles?" and he said, " 'Maxwell's Silver Hammer.'" He said, "I sat in the studio for three weeks while McCartney did the vocals and by the time we were done, I hated him." (laughs) Of course that's not what broke them up, but it was like a straw that broke the camels back.

Jack Douglas (producer, *Double Fantasy*): I'd ride home with him because I only lived two blocks from him. And he'd start talking, you know, reminiscing about things. We'd listen to the radio and if a Beatles song came on, he'd talk about it. He'd remind me that the Beatles were *his* band and how much he loved those guys. He was pissed off at George [Harrison] for writing a book [*I Me Mine*] and not really mentioning him. You know, "How can he write a book about his life and not mention me?"

L-R: Yoko Ono, Hugh McCracken, Jack Douglas, Tony Davilio, Tony Levin. Foreground: John Lennon.

Lights, Camera, Action!

According to an entry in George Small's 1980 log, on August 18, 1980, from 2:00 p.m. to 4:30 a.m., a video crew led by director Jay Dubin assembled inside the Hit Factory to shoot footage of the recording sessions. Dubin and crew captured the band running through two *Double Fantasy* numbers: "I'm Losing You" and "I'm Moving On," along with a batch of rock and roll oldies, including the Beatles' "She's a Woman," Elvis Presley's Sun Records jewel "Mystery Train," "Stay" by Maurice Williams, the Gene Vincent classic "Be-Bop-A-Lula," "Dream Lover" by Bobby Darin, Eddie Cochran's "C'mon Everybody," "I'm a Man," and others. To this day, the whereabouts of the footage remains a mystery.

Jay Dubin (director, *Double Fantasy* video shoot): I'd done work doing all the Crazy Eddie commercials, these crazy and wild commercials. Crazy Eddie's was an electronics store and he also had a number of record stores. He was the king of late-night commercials. He would come on TV and scream, "Crazy Eddie's prices are insane!" (laughs) I knew Jack Douglas, we were in Brazil together and were trying to put together a rock and roll show for Warner Brothers.

Jack Douglas (producer, *Double Fantasy*): I was gonna do the first rock concert at the biggest arena in Brazil. I knew Jay had done the Crazy Eddie commercials and knew he was the kind of guy I would get along with to do videos. John was saying, "We need video of these sessions." I told John, "I know a guy."

Jay Dubin (director, *Double Fantasy* video shoot): I was one of the few people at the time that had a mobile phone—it looked like a police walkie-talkie. I remember standing in front of the Waverly Theater on Sixth Avenue and it's John Lennon on the phone and he said Jack Douglas wants me to do this video with them. I didn't believe it was John Lennon, I thought it was someone pulling a joke on me. But he said, "I really am John Lennon." He must have gotten this a lot (laughs). "Okay, let me sing a little bit of a song for you" and he did. So he convinced me it was him and then he put Jack on the phone. They wanted me to document a *Double Fantasy* session. Remember, this was before MTV. They didn't call them music videos, they called them clips. They wanted me to shoot a session over at the Hit Factory. Then I put together a crew. I ran the camera. I called Ritchie Fliegler, who used to play guitar with Lou Reed, to do sound. Lucas George was the gaffer, he's now gone on to become a big producer, now he's doing the TV show *Life* for NBC, and I hired Freddie Schifferman as one of the grips.

Jon Smith (assistant engineer, *Double Fantasy*): The footage was being shot for use for the first single, as far as I remember. The video guys were taking a lot of time to set up and everyone was just standing around with their instruments. It was extremely boring and was taking forever, so someone started playing an old rock and roll song. Suddenly, the whole band just took off and started jamming on old songs. They continued playing for about half an hour or so. It was very cool.

Jay Dubin (director, *Double Fantasy* video shoot): It was a one-day session.

Jack Douglas (producer, *Double Fantasy*): They shot all day and into the night. John was way into it. He just loved it. He was in the booth rockin' away with a camera in front of him.

Hugh McCracken (guitar, *Double Fantasy*): John was clowning around and having a great time. We were playing live to a finished track so it sounded monstrous. We were doubling the track and it sounded really big. The audio from that video shoot is floating around. At one time during the school John made a funny comment when asked if he wanted to look at some of the footage, he said, "I know what I look like, a fuckin' bird!" (laughs)

Tony Levin (bass, *Double Fantasy*): Though it was late in the day, after tracking, he absolutely lit up when the camera went on him to perform the vocal. Suddenly gone was the family man, the producer . . . the performer side of John turned on, as if by a switch, and it was the first I'd seen of that.

Jay Dubin (director, *Double Fantasy* video shoot): They were playing songs from the album and also jamming. John was terrific.

Andy Newmark (drummer, *Double Fantasy*): Hugh McCracken sent me a cassette of a recording of all of us in the studio with John during the *Double Fantasy* sessions. It's really funny stuff and very typical of what went on with him a lot of the time while we were in the recording studio. It was recorded on a day when there was a crew filming us recording one of John's new songs on *Double Fantasy*. The film crew arrived and needed an hour to get set up and ready to film us; however, they needed us to keep playing so they could figure out their camera shots and all that technical stuff. John didn't want to wear out this new song of his, playing it over and over, before we taped it for real for the cameras. So, this was the perfect opportunity for John to start goofing around, talking nonsense, playing old rock and roll songs by all kinds of people, and singing stupid lyrics instead of the real lyrics, which I love to do, as well. The film crew was hysterical observing all this. I have a recording of all of us rehearsing "Starting Over." It must have come from that tape machine that was running constantly in the studio. John sings the first line of "Starting Over," "It's been so long since we've been apart, my feet are hurting, I start to fart." This was so typical of him. I love that he could make fun of his own lyrics and really have fun like that. John's just talking and laughing and singing complete nonsense, which he could do really well. This goes on for the better part of an hour on the cassette. When I hear it, I smile because John sounds so happy and I was really happy, too.

Jay Dublin (director, *Double Fantasy* video shoot): During that shoot we had a little problem with the camera. The cameras were not as robust as they are today, especially the handheld ones. When the camera would heat up there'd be this color overlapping. So when we were shooting at one point the image had a green ghosting effect. I told John, "I gotta have this guy adjust the camera." And he said, "Don't worry about it, I'm John Lennon, everyone will think it's art and you'll get an award for it." (laughs) I watched back some of the footage at the session and it looked great.

Ritchie Fliegler: (sound engineer, *Double Fantasy* video shoot): After I had the sound set up, I pretty much had nothing to do. So I sat in the back of the room and watched the shoot. At some point they ordered dinner. When it came time to eat, John went out into the studio and everybody else stayed in the control room. John sat down at the piano and I wandered in. He saw me and said, "You don't belong here, what's your story?" I told him I was a guitar player and that I'd played with Lou Reed and John Cage. He said, "Okay, sit down." So the two of us sat together on the piano bench and talked for a half an hour. He started talking about playing guitar and how he wished he was a better player. We got into that source of frustration. No matter how good you are, you're always kind of frustrated at what you can't do. I believe Duke Ellington said, "It's not what you can do that creates style, it's what you can't do that creates your style." I said, "Let's face it, John, you're not a great guitar player, but you're John Lennon and you can do other things well" and he started laughing.

He also talked about how his songs in the Beatles were the ones that got the production treatment. He said, "When I brought 'Strawberry Fields' in, it was a regular song. Paul's songs were always just played straight." He said, "I can't even listen to 'Strawberry Fields' anymore." I said, "If you allow me to respectfully disagree with you, I think it came out pretty well." (laughs) I kept thinking, I'm sitting here with John Lennon! In his mind he was talking to me like I was an equal, but not in mine (laughs) and that really struck me about him.

Jay Dubin (director, *Double Fantasy* video shoot): Freddie Schif-ferman, who was one of our grips and a real character, sat down and started talking with John like they were friends for a hundred years. As a joke, he'd say to him, "John, do you do weddings and bar mitzvahs?" John said, "Oh sure, Freddie" and laughed. I remember that John sat at the piano and the two of them sang a quick chorus of "Feelings" together. It was hilarious. These guys were really hit-ting it off. Had we shot another day, they'd have probably gone out for beers together.

George Small (keyboards, *Double Fantasy*): The day of the video shoot was the longest day of the session. It started around noon and ended around three in the morning. They shot footage of us playing together and then footage of each individual band member. Un-fortunately, I was last on the list and wound up staying till the wee hours of the morning. I remember Jack [Douglas] wanted me to do this Chico Marx piano glissando trick that he did in all of the Marx Brothers films. It was tough to do for me, but Jack could pull it off.

Lee DeCarlo (engineer, *Double Fantasy*): They were shooting in the control room and we were all fooling around with the faders. At the end of the song as we were fading everything out on the rough mix, we were exhausted from this long day, and all of us—John included—fell on the floor while pulling the faders down (laughs).

Stan Vincent (Jack Douglas's business partner): At the end of the session I turned around to the video director and said, "Give me all the tapes." So the guy gives me these reel-to-reel videotapes. John and Yoko are walking out and they're headed for the elevator. The door started to close, I run to the elevator, hold the door open, and take these tapes and thrust them at John and said, "Here, take these!" And he turns around and hands them back to me and goes, "No, you hold 'em." (laughs) And I take them and go, "No, no, no, here!" And that's the last I saw of those tapes (laughs).

Jon Smith (assistant engineer, *Double Fantasy*): John told us that he watched them and he said he hated the video so he destroyed the tapes. He told us that he pulled the tape out of their shells and flushed them down the toilet.

Jack Douglas (producer, *Double Fantasy*): He was tired of being the fat Beatle. He was really in shape. We used to call John "Skinny Head" when he would pull his hair back in a ponytail and his face looked narrow. He did it that day for the video and he shouldn't have. When he saw the results, he went crazy. He just hated it.

Jay Dubin (director, Double Fantasy video shoot): I understand that a little footage of Yoko in the studio doing a song ("I'm Moving On") was used for a documentary done on her back in the eighties [*Yoko Ono: Then & Now*].

Jack Douglas (producer, *Double Fantasy*): I saw all the footage and it was pretty incredible stuff. It was beautiful footage. The audio's from my hidden mic tapes.

Hidden Mics

Throughout the *Double Fantasy* sessions, a tape machine was constantly rolling, capturing the complete dialogue and musical moments from these historic recording sessions.

Tony Davilio (arranger, *Double Fantasy*): If you walked into the control room, to the extreme right there was this little closet. The door wasn't facing out, it was on the side. Jon Smith or Julie Last, the assistant engineers, would open it every few hours. Turns out there were two Studer twenty-four-tracks in there so I thought they were cleaning the machines. There were hidden mics throughout the studio and the tape was constantly going. Hours and hours of those sessions are taped. When I think back, I can remember Jack looking at Jon or Julie and they'd go into that little closet. I thought he was giving them a cue to clean the tape heads. What did I know? (laughs)

Jack Douglas (producer, *Double Fantasy*): On the first or second day of recording, John said to me, "It's a shame we're not recording everything that's going on. Not just the music, but we should hear all the dialogue, and what you guys are saying in the control room." That day I didn't go home with him.

Jon Smith (assistant engineer, *Double Fantasy*): At the beginning of the project, Jack came to Julie and me and he said, "Here's what we're going to do. Anytime that John is on microphone, I want a tape machine running with only that mic being recorded. We'll do this through the whole project and at the end, we're going to hand him the tapes as a gift."

Jack Douglas (producer, *Double Fantasy*): We planted mics everywhere.

Julie Last (assistant engineer, *Double Fantasy*): Jack knew this was a historic session and so we had a reel-to-reel tape machine running constantly to capture all the bits of talking and rehearsing and hanging out. The machine was set to run very slow so we could get a lot of time onto each reel. One of my jobs was to keep loading tapes onto the machine.

Jack Douglas (producer, *Double Fantasy*): We had all these mics going to this big mono machine with giant reels on it, going at a very slow speed so you hardly had to change tapes, almost like a transcription tape.

Jon Smith (assistant engineer, *Double Fantasy*): Julie and I were responsible for making sure that the mic was always bussed to a certain tape machine and that we always had a tape ready to go.

Andy Newmark (drummer, *Double Fantasy*): There was always a lot of talking and fooling around going on in the studio and it was all recorded, too. Jack Douglas felt John was important and he might as well document it all. But that's exactly how it was for the Beatles for many years. Everything they said, everything they thought, every move they made was under the microscope of the press and the fans. They couldn't do anything without being scrutinized and it wasn't that different for them in 1980. People wanted to hear whatever John was talking about. That's a great burden. I think it's why he joked around so much and kept things light and funny. What else can one do when every word out of their mouth is being analyzed and dissected by obsessive-compulsive fans all over the world? No one wants to be taken that seriously and watched that closely twenty-four hours a day.

Earl Slick (guitar, *Double Fantasy*): They recorded everything that was going on in the studio all the time. There's got to be miles of tape that people haven't heard yet. There was a two-track machine running twenty-four/seven in that friggin' place. There's us jamming on songs like "Be-Bop-A-Lula," "Rip It Up," and "Mystery Train." There's a number of things that got recorded with us jamming on songs. We'd do like half a song or a piece of a song. A lot of it happened during the sessions that were being videotaped. Things just weren't all that businesslike in there. If you recorded a record it wasn't like you went to the office and said, "Today's tasks are . . ." He went in and said, "We're gonna do this song called 'Woman.'" But that didn't necessarily mean that's all we did all day. It was loose. The idea was it keeps a good, loose atmosphere going on where you're not treating it as a project. We worked almost business hours. There were never these twelve, fifteen, and twenty-hour days in there. You weren't leaving the studio at three o'clock in the morning.

Jon Smith (assistant engineer, *Double Fantasy*): One day when we were mixing at the Record Plant, John came into the control room and came over to me and said, "Tell me something. I notice there's always a tape machine rolling and it's always in record and the meter seems like it's moving with our voices. What's going on?" Now I was sworn to secrecy so I told him it was a machine we used for slap echo, but he wasn't buying it and he was getting angry. He pressed me harder and harder so I finally looked at Jack and said, "Jack, help!" That's when we finally told him what we were doing. There was a time when the government was trying to deport John and the FBI was tapping his phones and it all made him a little suspicious. Once he knew there was an innocent explanation for it, he thought it was a great idea.

Jack Douglas (producer, *Double Fantasy*): For his birthday I gave him wireless Sennheiser headphones and a stack of cassettes. He said, "What's this?" And I said, "It's what you asked for." It was the tapes of all the sessions and he listened to it. He loved that kind of stuff. He thought it was the coolest thing. He had the cassettes and the reels went to Studio One [John and Yoko's company].

Julie Last (assistant engineer, *Double Fantasy*): I believe Yoko ended up with those tapes and ultimately, after John was gone, put together the most interesting bits as an audio diary.

Sonic Architecture

With the album in the can, mixing would commence at the Record Plant.

James Ball (assistant mix engineer, *Double Fantasy*): I'd been working at the Record Plant a little over two years when early one morning I got a call to come into the office. They informed me that I would be working with John and Yoko and Jack and Lee, mixing their new record. This was very important to Roy [Cicala] as he had worked on John's previous solo albums and as the owner of the Record Plant he wanted them to have the best possible experience. We worked in the new mix room on the tenth floor, which had just been beautifully renovated. It had a glassed-in pyramid ceiling and the all-oak room was quite spectacular with city views. Roy loved that room and the acoustics were amazing.

Now, any normal day at the Record Plant during this period you might find Aerosmith, KISS, Bruce Springsteen, or David Bowie working in various rooms. There were four studios and two trucks for live recording. We were not ruffled by celebrity, but this was John Lennon, and you could tell the entire staff was very excited. I walked into the mix room and everything was sparkling and the lighting was perfect. Some extra equipment had been brought in to accommodate the session, including two sixteen-track, two-inch Ampex machines and an extra sixteen-channel API board that floated around mostly on the trucks. Our maintenance engineers, Steve Barish and Michael Guthrie, had tweaked every machine in the room and connected all the gear that Jack and Lee had requested. We all felt a very special anticipation waiting for John and Yoko to show up. They arrived with a small party of handlers and some equipment of their own. There was an espresso machine, a cappuccino machine, lots of fine chocolate, sunflower seeds, and a few cartons of Gauloises cigarettes. You knew something special was going to happen.

John would come in around noon and we'd start working with him. Yoko would show up around five after the office closed. She'd be tired, so she'd lie down on the couch with a pillow and blanket and just listen. Occasionally she would chime in with her comments. She had very definite ideas about the way her songs should sound and strong ideas about her vocals—when the ad-libs should come in, how loud her voice should be.

There wasn't any BS about John and Yoko. There was a sense of urgency to get to the truth and speak the truth. Lennon sang "Gimme Some Truth"; that's the way they were. They didn't mince words. They knew what they wanted, they knew what they liked, in both life and in music.

We were there working at the Record Plant for about ten days. We'd mixed "Starting Over," "Woman," "Watching the Wheels," "Kiss Kiss Kiss," and I think "Beautiful Boy." Then we'd move downstairs to mix in Studio B because Lee wanted to work on an automated console. Yoko wasn't there that night, which was unusual. Around 10:30 p.m., John disappeared. I came in the next day. Lee and Jack arrived, but John didn't show up. Late in the afternoon we called and tried to find him. Then Yoko didn't show up, either. Eventually Jack and Lee left, as well. At around 10:00 p.m., someone in Lennon's camp called and said, "Get the tapes ready, we're moving back to the Hit Factory." So I called Roy Cicala, who was the studio owner. "What do I do?" He said, "Don't give them the tapes." But about an hour later he said it was okay to hand them over the tapes.

John in the control room with engineer Lee DeCarlo.

Picture Perfect

Shot by renowned Japanese photographer Kishin Shinoyama, the front cover of the *Double Fantasy* album portrayed the couple locked in a passionate kiss. It remains one of the most enduring and iconic images in rock and roll. However, prior to coming up with that concept, John and Yoko had another idea in mind.

George Small (keyboards, *Double Fantasy*): The original concept for the cover was supposed to be a photograph or painting of Robert and Elizabeth Barrett Browning with their faces cut out and John and Yoko's superimposed over them. It was gonna have that sepia, early photography kind of look.

Yoko Ono: "Let Me Count the Ways" was by Elizabeth Browning and "Grow Old Beside Me" was by Robert Browning. Before we came up with those two songs, "Let Me Count the Ways" and "Grow Old with Me," back when we were living in England in Ascot, John was reading this book about Robert and Elizabeth Browning. (*Author's note: John's lyrics for "Grow Old with Me" are borrowed from Browning's poem "Rabbi Ben Ezra" written in 1864.*)

He said to me, "We're just a reincarnation of Robert and Elizabeth Browning (laughs)." I said, "Maybe." It was very funny because Elizabeth was older than Robert and I was older than John.

Kishin Shinoyama (photographer, *Double Fantasy* front and back cover): After John and Yoko finished with the recording of the record, we decided to shoot the cover in the glow of sunset. I was watching their loving attitude, so I proposed to them the idea of the kiss and that photo was picked for the front cover of the album. It was shot at a bench in Central Park. The back cover photo was shot at the crossing street in front of the Dakota where John and Yoko were living.

Yoko Ono: We shot that photo with us kissing, which would go on to be used as the front cover of *Double Fantasy* and we thought it looked great. But we weren't that sure about it. When we showed that photo to our record company they said, "No, no, the photo on the cover has to be John looking like a bachelor. We want a single photo of John on the cover. You can't be kissing." So that's when we decided we were gonna do it (laughs), because both of us were rebellious people. John said, "From now on, we'll only take photos of you and me looking at each other."

Double Fantasy

In the summer of 1980 while in Bermuda, John visits the botanical gardens and spots a freesia flower named "Double Fantasy," which he decides is the perfect title for the new record.

John Lennon: (on the origin of *Double Fantasy*) It's a flower, a type of freesia, but what it means to us is that if two people picture the same image at the same time, that is the secret. You can be together, but projecting two different images, and either whoever's the stronger at the time will get his or her fantasy fulfilled or you will get nothing but mishmash.[19]

Finishing Touches

Subtitled "A Heart Play," the tracks on *Double Fantasy* would act as a musical dialogue between John and Yoko. Rather than stacking all of John's songs on one side of the album and Yoko's on the other, the album was consciously sequenced where a John song would be followed by a Yoko tune.

Ed Rosenblatt (president, Geffen Records): We thought the record would flow better if it featured John's songs on one side and Yoko's on the other, but that didn't fly. They had their own ideas of how to do it.

David Sheff (writer, *Playboy*): The sequencing of the record wasn't firmed up at the beginning; it evolved. I remember them with their list of songs, shifting them around. We'd be sitting with them in the apartment in the morning and John might go, "Maybe this song should go before this one. Maybe this song shouldn't go on *Double Fantasy*, maybe we should save this for the next album?" So that was pretty exciting, too. They had this idea of a story unfolding and even thought it was somewhat formed, and they knew "Starting Over" would lead off the record; there was some question about how things would go after that.

Jack Douglas (producer, *Double Fantasy*): We were just about finished mixing the record. Yoko, John, and I sat in a room and we were talking about how we wanted to sequence the album. She said, "Why don't we all throw our sequences into this hat and somewhere between the three of us we'll come up with the right one." We said, "That sounds good." I throw mine in, John throws in his, and Yoko throw hers in. She said, "Okay, let's look." She pulls out one and sees it's mine. She's reading and goes, "No," and throws it down. She picks up John's next, goes "No," and puts it down. Then she says to us, "What's wrong with this?" I pick up John's and he picks up mine and ours were really close. It was all of John's songs on side A and all of Yoko's songs on side B. She said, "No way. If you wanna listen to John, you've gotta hear Yoko." And John said, "She's right," and she was. So the way it was sequenced was a John song would be followed by a Yoko song. If the album wasn't sequenced that way, what would have happened is people would have only listened to John's songs and not have given her songs a chance.

David Geffen (Geffen Records): The idea behind sequencing John's songs with Yoko's was John's decision.

Yoko Ono: The record is subtitled "A Heart Play" because we thought we were presenting a play with the songs showing off various sides of people's emotion. It all has to do with heart.

Jack Douglas (producer, *Double Fantasy*): *Double Fantasy* was intended to be a play and there was a dialogue and we had to have this dialogue between the two of them. Ultimately, she was right.

George Small (keyboards, *Double Fantasy*): It was such a giving gesture on John's part to alternate her songs with his. It's all part of that Robert Browning connection. John and Yoko thought they were the reincarnation of Robert and Elizabeth Barrett Browning, who were poets from the Victorian era. It's integral to the whole idea of the *Double Fantasy* concept. Yoko had called John when he was in Bermuda and mentioned a Robert Browning poem, called "Grow Old Beside Me." That poem inspired John to write "Grow Old with Me," which was supposed to be cut for *Double Fantasy*, but was held back for the next record.

By the Numbers

John, Yoko, and the participants in the making of the record provide the backstory behind the writing and recording of the songs that comprised *Double Fantasy*.

John Lennon: We cut twenty-two tracks in ten days, and we just zapped out these twenty-two tracks and got it down to fourteen.[20]

Stan Vincent (Jack Douglas's business partner): He wanted to tell people, "This is a family album, this isn't about protest."

John Lennon: They were all dialogue songs, meaning that we were writing it as if it were a play, and we were two characters in it. What we sing about in the record, and the songs, are real diaries of how we feel. We're not presenting ourselves as the perfect couple. . . . We have our problems, we have our doubts, but we're trying. We want to stay together. When I was singing and working with her, I was visualizing all the people of my age group for the sixties being in their thirties or forties now, just like me, and having wives and children, and having gone through everything together. I'm singing to them. I'm saying, Here I am now, how are you? How's your relationship going? Did you get through it all? Wasn't the seventies a drag? Let's try to make the eighties good 'cause it's still up to us to make what we can of it. It's not out of our control. I still believe in love, peace.[21]

(Just Like) Starting Over

John Lennon: All through the taping of "Starting Over," I was calling what I was doing "Elvis Orbison": "I want you I need you, only the lonely." I'm a born-again rocker, I feel *that* refreshed, and I'm going right back to my roots. It's like Dylan doing *Nashville Skyline*, except I don't have any Nashville, you know, being from Liverpool. So I go back to the records I know—Elvis and Roy Orbison and Gene Vincent and Jerry Lee Lewis.[22] It was the one where the musicians got very loose because it was such simple rock and roll, there was no problem . . . some of the other tracks are stronger, I mean like, "Losing You" might be a stronger piece of material, but "Starting Over" was the best way to start over.[23] I wrote "Starting Over" for Yoko, but afterwards I realized it's a message to all women, a plea for all of us—men and woman—to start over. Sexism is such a big issue, and we haven't even begun to deal with it. There are all kinds of inequities in the world—this race versus that race, this country versus that country, but it's always women at the bottom.[24]

Yoko Ono: We knew that song would be the first single. I love "Starting Over," but when I hear it now it just chokes me up a bit because (sighs) it's how we felt at the time. We really thought that we were starting over and it didn't work out that way.

Lee DeCarlo (engineer, *Double Fantasy*): His message was "Starting Over." He'd gotten rid of a whole bunch of contractual obligations. He'd raised his child to the age of five. He believed that anything you're gonna do to your kid you need to do in the first five years.

Andy Newmark (drummer, *Double Fantasy*): It's my favorite track on the record. When we recorded "Starting Over," I thought that the song's 12/8 shuffle groove, which was the only groove on the record like it, and very reminiscent of old fifties rock and roll, was very unique. It has a great feel. We were seventies cats playing that fifties groove and it came out different than the old days. That's what happens.

George Small (keyboards, *Double Fantasy*): We did that song in two or three takes. It came fast. In a sense, the song kind of played itself—the piano playing, the triplets, Andy's backbeat, Tony's great bass part, and John, Hugh, and Earl's guitar playing. The production is also great.

Hugh McCracken (guitar, *Double Fantasy*): I came up with the guitar lick in the chorus of "Starting Over" and it's something that I'm very proud of. When I first came up with the lick it wasn't the way it turned out on the record. One take prior it wasn't as good or complete as it wound up being.

Earl Slick (guitar, *Double Fantasy*): There was no doubt that this was gonna be one of the big singles.

Andy Newmark (drummer, *Double Fantasy*): Everyone was kind of dancing and swaying to the playback of "Starting Over" in the control room. I know I certainly was. It just felt so good when that track was turned up loud. I remember standing next to John by the board and when it stopped I looked at him and said, "Hey, man, this is special." He looked at me and said real innocently, "Oh yeah, do you think so, why is that?" I said, "Man, it's got that magic, that groove thing, the thing that musicians get off on." I suppose that one could debate whether it's a great song or not, but as a backing track from a musician's point of view, it's totally smoking. All musicians know that feeling in the studio when a track is playing back that has that indescribable thing and attitude, jumping out of the speakers at you. From a drummer's point of view, "Starting Over" had that "thing." No question. It was poppin', man. When it was turned up loud, you would have to be in a coma if you weren't tapping your foot to it. It turned out to be the first single. John did his Elvis impersonation, which really has tons of personality. His lead vocal is fantastic on that.

Lee DeCarlo (engineer, *Double Fantasy*): On "Starting Over" we had the room set up in a different way in order to make all of the sounds on the album not sound identical. We would move stuff around. We'd move the drums to a different part of the room, change the amps.

Tony Davilio (arranger, *Double Fantasy*): All the female background parts on "Starting Over" were originally horn parts (imitates), the "doo doo" parts. I had to sit there and give the singers the notes for their three-part harmonies.

James Ball (assistant mix engineer, *Double Fantasy*): That middle eight piece in "Starting Over" before the drum break where you hear that swirling sound, that's all done with a process called real-time tape flanging, a technique that Jimi Hendrix popularized. It was about 11:30 p.m. and Yoko was pushing to have the song mixed by midnight. It was tied in with her numerology beliefs. Lee was trying to get all the edits done and I remember he looked up at me and rolled his eyes at the "numerology" mention, but there *was* a sense of urgency.

Lee DeCarlo (engineer, *Double Fantasy*): I did an edit on the drum fill and when I cut it together, I missed the edit and had repeated one of the ending drum fills.

James Ball (assistant mix engineer, *Double Fantasy*): We heard the repeated drum part and thought, Oh my God, we're never gonna finish this by midnight!

Lee DeCarlo (engineer, *Double Fantasy*): Everybody went, "Oh no!" and I yelled, "I like it better!"

James Ball (assistant mix engineer, *Double Fantasy*): John chimed in, "That's brilliant! Play that again!"

Lee DeCarlo (engineer, *Double Fantasy*): It was a bad edit, but it was just one of those little gifts.

Andy Newmark (drummer, *Double Fantasy*): It sounds great on the record, but I don't think I could actually re-create that fill. I would need three hands. Funnily enough, some young drummers have learned how to duplicate the fill on the record and have written me about it. Amazing.

Jon Smith (assistant engineer, *Double Fantasy*): In the fade, you hear a flight attendant announcing that the plane is approaching the runway. It's a woman's voice announcing, "World Airlines flight, (maybe 'flight twelve') with service to . . ." I think it came off a sound effects record. He had originally wanted the sound of a supersonic jet landing and I remember calling all over the country, trying to find somebody who had that sound effect. We never got it, so instead we used the flight attendant. John had warned us that we had to finish the mix by a certain time of the day. According to Yoko, the stars would be in perfect alignment (or something) and if we didn't finish by this time it wouldn't be good. We saw the deadline approaching and we were working like crazy to get it done in time. Finally, with just a few minutes to go, the mix was all done except for one detail, the bell at the front of "Starting Over." John had brought the bell from home. I believe it was a special bell, maybe a wishing bell or something.

John Lennon: If you remember, at the beginning of "Mother" [*Plastic Ono Band*] . . . it's a church bell which I slowed down to thirty-three, so it's really like a horror movie and that was the death knell of the whole Mother-Father Freudian trip . . . I put it on *Double Fantasy* to show the likeness and difference of the long, long trip from "Mother" to "Starting Over."[25]

Lee DeCarlo (engineer, *Double Fantasy*): We used these Tibetan bells at the beginning that were a bazillion years old.

Jon Smith (assistant engineer, *Double Fantasy*): We ran and got a mic and hooked it up. Time was running out so we really had to move. We recorded the bell and put it into the mix and finished with just a minute to spare. We laughed with joy at making it in time. I'm not sure, but seem to remember John calling Yoko to tell her we made it and then the session was over.

Kiss Kiss Kiss

Yoko Ono: Some people thought a woman shouldn't come on and say "kiss me," that kind of thing. Those were the days when guys were still thinking that way. You know, "Don't come on to us." It was the thinking that women should not be aggressive in terms of sexuality. Just the fact that the song said (recites lyrics), "Kiss kiss kiss kiss me, love." It wasn't said aggressively, like (says boldy), "Kiss me!" It was just "Kiss kiss kiss kiss me, love." Something like that was threatening to the guys. Can you imagine? (laughs) It's kind of a feminist song in a way. I wanted to write a song that was me.

George Small (keyboards, *Double Fantasy*): That's the strongest statement of Yoko's songs in my opinion. Maybe that's why it's the second song on the record. That used to mean more in the days of records. Nowadays people can skip around at will on a CD. That song really impressed me a lot.

Jack Douglas (producer, *Double Fantasy*): When we needed some unique guitar playing, Hugh McCracken and Earl came up with some really cool stuff.

Hugh McCracken (guitar, *Double Fantasy*): That song brings a smile to my face. It's got great punk energy.

Earl Slick (guitar, *Double Fantasy*): That's me playing lead guitar on "Kiss Kiss Kiss." I was starting to experiment with little pedals and I've got a feeling I used something weird on that.

Jon Smith (assistant engineer, *Double Fantasy*): We usually built a little wall of sound baffles around singers to cut down on room tone. It was almost always facing towards the window of the control room so we could communicate with the singer. When it was time to record Yoko's orgasm parts, we faced it to the side of the studio so that we would have no view of her.

Yoko Ono: I was lying down on the floor in the studio to sing that part at the end so I was able to have some privacy. It was funny.

Jon Smith (assistant engineer, *Double Fantasy*): We put a rug down and the microphone was down by the floor. She laid down there so we couldn't see her and we hit record and she started making these orgasmic sounds. We were all in the control room with our jaws hanging open. It was amazing. It was shocking. It was also funny.

Tony Davilio (arranger, *Double Fantasy*): At the end of it, all of a sudden she went into that primal scream. John jumped up and screamed, "Yeah, Mother!" He really loved it. He was Yoko's champion. He really believed in her.

George Small (keyboards, *Double Fantasy*): "Kiss Kiss Kiss" was revolutionary. When she recorded that part of the performance, the "Yokogasm," she wanted the vocal booth to be dark. She wrapped herself in a blanket and did her orgasmic thing. She had worked with people like Meyer Kupferman and John Cage, so she had a background in the real avant-garde scene.

Tony Davilio (arranger, *Double Fantasy*): I played some kind of weird keyboard sound on "Kiss Kiss Kiss."

Cleanup Time

John Lennon: The song came from a talk with Jack Douglas before the session. We were talkin' about cleanin' up and gettin' out of drug and alcohol and those kind of things—not me personally, but people in general. He said, "Well, it's cleanup time, right?" I said, "It sure is," and that was the end of the conversation. I went straight to the piano and started boogyin' and "Cleanup Time" came out.[26]

Jack Douglas (producer, *Double Fantasy*): "Cleanup Time" was the most challenging song of John's to record. I mentioned to John in the limo that everybody was at this point in their lives, a lot had been smoking, drinking, or doing coke. I said, "It seems to me that a lot of people are cleaning up now." And he said, "Yeah, I'm doing the same."

George Small (keyboards, *Double Fantasy*): Harmonically, it's very adventurous. I forgot how tricky it was. It's a fantastic track. I love the horn parts on it. It has a sort of "Tomorrow Never Knows" ending, that slice of life mélange, snippets of musique concrète.

Hugh McCracken (guitar, *Double Fantasy*): That's a funky track. Earl's guitar playing shines on that song.

Earl Slick (guitar, *Double Fantasy*): I played the solo live. The weird thing is for some reason, John might have yelled out for me to do the solo there. It's on the basic track; it's not a redo or overdub. I love the song.

Jack Douglas (producer, *Double Fantasy*): The song was built around Tony's bass riff.

Jon Smith (assistant engineer, *Double Fantasy*): When we had any downtime, Tony would pick up his bass and play this little riff.

Tony Levin (bass, *Double Fantasy*): At that time, I was playing with a technique called hammer-ons. I'd learned it from a drummer. It was a little unusual at the time. I was obnoxiously practicing that technique between takes on every session that I did. At some point in one of the sessions when trying to think of an intro for "Cleanup Time," John looked at me and said, "Why don't you come up with an intro and do that thing you do."

Tony Levin (bass, *Double Fantasy*): I'm not really proud of it because I'm a little embarrassed that I must have been driving everybody crazy, practicing those chordal things on the bass (laughs). I was honored that he cared enough about my playing and was captivated enough to even think about asking me to do an introduction for one of his songs.

Lee DeCarlo (engineer, *Double Fantasy*): In that song you hear background vocal, "Got to clean up, clean up." I used the horns to trigger a vocoder. I think I sang "Got to clean up" so it made the horns sound like vocals. They did the same thing on "Bohemian Rhapsody" by Queen; the sound of all those background vocals is being done by a vocoder. You play a synthesizer, you sing into a microphone, and it picks up the characteristics of the chords and turns it into vocals. The background vocals in there are actually the horn players being turned into voices.

Give Me Something

Yoko Ono: I put one song on the record that was experimental in the sense of musical construction and that was "Give Me Something."

Jack Douglas (producer, *Double Fantasy*): We really wanted something that was wild and up tempo and gave Andy Newmark a chance to play hard. I used to go out before Andy came to a session and leave two pencils on his snare drum. Then when he came in I would walk him over to the drums and talk to him about what we were gonna do that day. I'd look down at the snare, pick up the pencils, and go, "No wonder you're playing so light. Maybe you should try sticks." (laughs) On that track it was a chance for him to really wack it out.

I'm Losing You

John Lennon: It came out of an overwhelming feeling of loss that went right back to the womb. One night, I couldn't get through to Yoko on the telephone and I felt completely disconnected . . . I think that's what the last five years were all about—to reestablish me for meself.[27] It was everything . . . losing one's mother, losing one's everything, losing everything you've ever lost is in that song . . . but sparked by the fact that I couldn't get through on the damned phone. "Can't even get you on the telephone."[28]

Yoko Ono: He wrote the song about being scared of losing me. "I'm Losing You" was written a little bit before the *Double Fantasy* time. Early on he had the song in a slightly different form. I remember John playing it on the piano and then he built it up on the basic thing that he had.

Jack Douglas (producer, *Double Fantasy*): It was my favorite track right from day one.

Yoko Ono: "I'm Losing You" is an incredible song. When I hear that it makes me almost faint. It's so beautifully written and the emotion is so powerful. I feel guilty, of course, as a woman, because he was scared he was gonna lose me.

Earl Slick (guitar, *Double Fantasy*): It's one of my favorite tracks on the record. It has that cutting, dark side of Lennon.

Jon Smith (assistant engineer, *Double Fantasy*): When cutting tracks, we finished "I'm Losing You" and then moved right into recording "I'm Moving On." They were always considered companion songs.

Hugh McCracken (guitar, *Double Fantasy*): That song was powerful. I remember John said, "Here's the next song." Then he played the riff from "I'm Losing You" and played the shit out of it. That riff just jumped out at us. It was simple and great, convincing and deliberate. It was easy for Earl and I to double that guitar part and do harmony on it.

Earl Slick (guitar, *Double Fantasy*): When we got the solo, John said, "I want you and Hughie to figure this out." What he had us do was, I'd play the first line and the second line would be Hughie. And the third line would be me and then the fourth line would be Hughie.

Hugh McCracken (guitar, *Double Fantasy*): Earl and I played that guitar solo in the control room with John and Jack sitting there. It was a great collaboration between Earl and I, it's just a beautiful memory for me.

Earl Slick (guitar, *Double Fantasy*): We each wrote parts of the solo. Then after we figured it out—John had some input, too, because he was in there when we did it—Hughie and I recorded it together. We doubled it for real. We played it together. And then we tracked it a number of times. John was pulling little Beatle tricks out of a hat. Apparently, he and George [Harrison] played a solo together on "Nowhere Man" through two small amps and there was a microphone sitting between the amps. So that's what we did. There was a microphone with the two amps facing each other. When you listen to the solo you can hear that swell of the guitars coming up.

Jon Smith (assistant engineer, *Double Fantasy*): The main electric guitar John used during the sessions was a Sardonyx guitar. It was a custom guitar made by a guy in Brooklyn. There were very few of them made. It looked like a Steinberger bass, but coming out of the body were these two metal aluminum struts. It made it look like the Starship *Enterprise* so John called it his "space guitar." I'm not sure when he got it, but he had it hanging on the wall next to his bed so he could pull it down and play it. I loved the sound of that guitar. He had an Eventide Harmonizer that someone had modified for him and he usually put the guitar through it. There was a specific setting that he loved and he didn't mess with it too much. You can really hear it wailing on the end of "I'm Losing You." A year or so later Earl Slick bought a Sardonyx guitar that was very similar to it and he later sold it to me. I now keep it next to my bed.

George Small (keyboards, *Double Fantasy*): That's an amazing track. It reminded me a lot of classic Lennon. The thing I noticed about the lyrics at the end, he sings "Don't wanna lose you now," it's a quote from the George Harrison song "Something." John sings it with that exact melody on the end of "I'm Losing You." I'm playing [Fender] Rhodes, organ, and synth on that.

Jon Smith (assistant engineer, *Double Fantasy*): John was always giving me things to research and get, a lot of sound effects. For the transition from "I'm Losing You" into "I'm Moving On," he thought it would be very cute to have a Morse code message in there that only people who knew Morse code could understand. As I recall, he wanted a Morse code that said "I love you Yoko." He told me that I had to get that. I don't remember if we actually did it or if it's just random Morse code that we found on a sound effects record.

I'm Moving On

Yoko Ono: "I'm Moving On" was a song I had already in my file. I wrote it during the period when John and I were separated or just about to get separated.

Earl Slick (guitar, *Double Fantasy*): There were some cool guitars on that song. I found Yoko's songs quite easy actually, because it was an open palette with her. She was open to ideas. And the weirder it was the more she liked it, which was perfect for me. Unbeknownst to myself at the time I do play more unconventionally than I think I do.

George Small (keyboards, *Double Fantasy*): "I'm Losing You" and "I'm Moving On" are linked. The guitar link that ends "I'm Losing You" or starts "I'm Moving On" (plays part on piano), they're quoting from "Miss You" by the Rolling Stones.

Beautiful Boy (Darling Boy)

John Lennon: I kept thinking, Well, I ought to be inspired to write about Sean. I mean, I ought to. I was going through a bit of that, and when I finally gave up thinking about writing a song about him, of course, the song came to me.[29] He didn't come out of my belly but, by God, I made his bones, because I've attended to every meal, and to how he sleeps, and to the fact that he swims like a fish. . . . I'm so proud of those things. He is my biggest pride, you see.[30]

Paul McCartney: I think it's a beautiful song. It's very moving to me.[31]

Jack Douglas (producer, *Double Fantasy*): I was happy to hear that "Beautiful Boy" was Paul McCartney's favorite John song, which made me feel really great because of the amount of work I'd done on it. There was a lot of emotion on that song.

Lee DeCarlo (engineer, *Double Fantasy*): It was a very heartfelt moment all the way through the basic tracks. A lot of crying went on. Everybody knew the significance of that song.

Stan Vincent (Jack Douglas's business partner): I gave John a big surprise. I got a big picture of Sean and had it blown up. In between the two speakers in the control room there was a TV monitor. Before the sessions even started, I climbed up there and put Sean's picture on the TV screen. It stayed there throughout the sessions.

John Lennon: I was guilty all through the making of *Double Fantasy*. We had his picture pinned in the studio 'cause I didn't want to lose contact with what I'd got. We had the picture up there all the time in between the speakers so whenever you're checking the stereo, he was looking at me all the time.[32]

Jon Smith (assistant engineer, *Double Fantasy*): There were a lot of times that John would talk to the picture.

Andy Newmark (drummer, *Double Fantasy*): It was clear John was really in love with Sean. I guess he missed out on raising his first son, Julian, because he was always on the road and the marriage split up, as well. He couldn't wait for Sean to show up at the Hit Factory after nursery school each day. John was always in an "up" mood in the studio, but he would go to the next level of "upness" and happiness when Sean would appear. He was always holding Sean in his lap or bouncing him on his knee asking, "Do you like this song?" John had spent the previous couple of years being, as he called it, a house husband. John told me that he was very hands-on when it came to raising Sean. He was involved in all the day-to-day stuff, which is very time-consuming. It seems that he really was enjoying that parental role at this point in his life. I think men start to become very good fathers from forty onwards. At forty, one has more of an overview and can nurture a child in the ways that matter. My stepdaughter Poppy knows Sean and from all that I hear from her, he sounds like a happy, well-adjusted, secure person. I have heard that from other people who know Sean, too. That's what happens when a child is loved. It would appear that Sean got enough love in those few years that he had his father around to see him through. I like that.

Lee DeCarlo (engineer, *Double Fantasy*): I asked him one time, "John, what are you most ashamed of, what's your biggest fuckup in your life?" I was sitting there with him for months and we were good friends. He said, "One day Yoko and I were in a hotel room and we were asleep and the phone rang. And this man said, 'Hello, Dad, I just bought a motorcycle.'" And right there he realized he had missed Julian's life. He hadn't been there for Julian while he was growing up. He regretted that more than anything else. "Beautiful Boy" was about how he did it right later in his life.

Jack Douglas (producer, *Double Fantasy*): That was one of my arrangements and it really came off, the way it was colored and structured. Sean came by at least three or four times a week and the song was played for him in the studio.

Lee DeCarlo (engineer, *Double Fantasy*): Sean heard the song in the studio and he was delighted.

George Small (keyboards, *Double Fantasy*): John played a piano part for me and I harmonized his original line, which had an Asian flair, and he didn't object. Listening to the album recently, that song hit me the strongest of anything I heard. It's got that great line, "Life is what happens when you're busy making other plans." I mean, who can ever forget that line? Originally, they wanted to hire a steel drum orchestra for the song. The number that was bandied about was twenty-plus. They finally decided that they could get the effect with one. He was a real Jamaican steel drum player and I had to teach him the song at the session.

Earl Slick (guitar, *Double Fantasy*): John and I played acoustic guitar on "Beautiful Boy" and Hughie played electric. I played John's black Yamaha acoustic guitar with a dragon on it.

Watching the Wheels

John Lennon: It's a song version of the love letter from John and Yoko. It's an answer to "What have you been doing?" "Well, I've been doing this—watchin' the wheels."[33]

Jack Douglas (producer, *Double Fantasy*): The original version of that song was like a Bob Dylan song. John said, "We need something that sounds circular." I said, "I know what we need, hammer dulcimer." He said, "Okay, can you find a hammer dulcimer player?" So I called the union and there wasn't a single one in all of New York. It was just the weirdest thing. Two days later I'm walking on Seventy-second Street and Columbus Avenue and this guy's sitting on the street, playing dulcimer, and people were throwing money in his box.

Tony Davilio (arranger, *Double Fantasy*): Jack heard this guy named Matthew Cunningham playing dulcimer on the street and he was good. This guy was a real hippie with stringy long hair. He was a typical street musician. They brought him in to play dulcimer on "Watching the Wheels." He came in looking pretty spaced out. When you play the dulcimer you sit in that Indian position on the floor. Jack told me, "Tony, go out there and make sure he's in tune." So I went over to the piano and plucked out some notes and he kept shaking his head and said, "That sounds sour, that's not in tune," but it was. So he's sitting there playing along with the track and the tape stops. John was standing up in the control room and said something to him over the talkback. Matt squinted his eyes, looking at him, and said, "What's your name?" And John gets back on the talkback and says "My name's John." This guy's just staring at him and goes, "Hi, John." And then John says, "Hi, Matt" and then I see them all laughing in there because this guy didn't know who he was (laughs). Apparently, he was the only person in the country who wouldn't know John Lennon (laughs).

John Lennon: He studied dulcimer with some famous person. He was very cosmic. He had to pick the right day from his astrologer to come in and do the session, which I thought was funny because we pick everything by numerology or astrology.[34]

Jack Douglas (producer, *Double Fantasy*): After he did the gig, he went home and called me two days later. "Wait a minute, did I just play for John Lennon?" And I said, "Yeah, you did." I think we paid him two hundred bucks (laughs). And he goes (indignantly), "Two hundred dollars!" I think John sent him to either Puerto Rico or maybe the Bahamas as a gift.

Jon Smith (assistant engineer, *Double Fantasy*): John went out to the electric piano to teach "Watching the Wheels" to the band. He spent a lot of time at the piano, going over and over it. He wasn't planning to play piano on the song, but Jack convinced him it would be really cool if he played one piano and George played the other one.

George Small (keyboards, *Double Fantasy*): "Watching the Wheels" really knocked me out, it's just an incredible song. There's just something special about that one. That's the most keyboard-oriented song on the record. It's not so guitar-driven as much of the other material. That's me on piano and John played a Yamaha electric grand. I'm also playing organ and all those Prophet 5 synthesizer parts, the thing that sounds like a French horn. On the ending part—where John sings, "I just had to let it go . . ."—he really made a big point of making sure that I had played that romantic piano line on the tag exactly that way. He told me he was in a bar one night and was listening to a piano player and that riff just stuck in his head. So he had to have that riff on the end of it.

Jack Douglas (producer, *Double Fantasy*): That's another song that reflects my production values. I slowed it down and got the circular feel to it that expresses what John was doing for those five years out of the business. He was very happy with the arrangement.

Earl Slick (guitar, *Double Fantasy*): That, lyrically, was one of my favorite songs on the record. It was an introspective Lennon thing, which I always loved. The songs where there wasn't a lot of guitar was harder, like "Watching the Wheels." There wasn't much for me to do on that song. You're not talking about your typical rock band. We had an arranger. We had a percussionist. We had a couple keyboard guys in there. There were three guitar players. So sometimes you'd have to fish for a part.

Yes, I'm Your Angel

Jack Douglas (producer, *Double Fantasy*): The introduction to it was so much fun for me, the sound effects of going through the park and into the Plaza Hotel. It's starting out like it's being played in the Palm Court. If you listen in headphones, it's really wild. It's like a sound movie. They go by this beggar man, which is John. What he'd always say to me was, "You know, you've got a lucky face." So he's in there saying that kind of gibberish.

George Small (keyboards, *Double Fantasy*): I played the stride piano style on that. It's a really cute song. It's Yoko's humor, which you don't hear a lot of times, because people get the mistaken impression that she's just dark and serious.

Woman

John Lennon: "Woman" came about because one sunny afternoon in Bermuda, it suddenly hit me. I saw what women do for us. Not just what my Yoko does for me, although I was thinking in those personal terms . . . in Bermuda, what suddenly dawned on me was everything I was taking for granted. Women really are the other half of the sky, as

I whisper at the beginning of the song. And it just sort of hit me like a flood, and it came out like that. The song reminds me of a Beatles track, but I wasn't trying to make it sound like that. I did it as I did "Girl" many years ago. So this is the grown-up version of "Girl."[35]

Yoko Ono: Every one of John's songs on the album is special, but they all make me feel weird and they choke me up. From a personal point of view, they're all too intense for me. Of course, personally, "Woman" just gets me.

Tony Davilio (arranger, *Double Fantasy*): John and I started playing guitar together and I began playing what I thought would be a good string part for "Woman" and he said (excitedly), "Yeah, write that down!" Then he said, "Maybe we could do this or that?" and whatever it was I would write it down. We had fun collaborating on the string parts.

Earl Slick (guitar, *Double Fantasy*): That's a very "Here, There, and Everywhere" kind of a song. It's great. As soon as I heard it, the first thing I thought was "Beatles." I loved all the songs we recorded. There wasn't anything I didn't like of John's or Yoko's. You have to understand something, you don't get an opportunity like that. Of all the guys on the planet, how many people got to play with the Beatles post-Beatles? Especially with Lennon. There wasn't a very long period of time between the end of the Beatles and the end of his life. Ten years. It's not long. And five of those years he wasn't active.

George Small (keyboards, *Double Fantasy*): I felt "Woman" and "Starting Over" were the most commercial tracks on the record. I thought it was beautiful and I loved playing it. I played piano and Fender Rhodes on that. That had a pop ballad sound to it, with those kinds of progressions that he'd used in previous songs he'd written.

Jack Douglas (producer, *Double Fantasy*): I thought that was gonna be a pop classic because it said everything about how a man feels about his wife or girlfriend. He wanted the song to have a pre-Beatles, early sixties feel, which is why I went with the background singers and then added the modulation at the end. I said, "This will give you that Righteous Brothers' 'You've Lost That Lovin' Feeling' feel," which he really liked.

Hugh McCracken (guitar, *Double Fantasy*): I came up with the arpeggiated guitar part in the chorus.

Andy Newmark (drummer, *Double Fantasy*): "Woman" is a beautiful song and lyric. He writes about love, but it's written from an older person's perspective, and not adolescent at all. We know he wrote plenty of the adolescent ones way back when, and good ones, too. "Woman" is a mature, forty-year-old man's version of love, in which he touches on the more-refined and sophisticated aspects of love. At forty years old, love is very different than when one is twenty. We can see, and appreciate deeper, more important, lasting aspects of a person when we're older. At twenty, love is a very physical thing. At forty, it's something else. What John says in "Woman" is very, very beautiful, no doubt honest, and shows that vulnerability in him that he has always been able to expose so beautifully. The backing track feels perfect. The background vocals gave it a Beatlesque feel.

Eric Troyer (background vocals, *Double Fantasy*): "Woman" had a Beatles feel and I think that's why Jack chose to have me work on the song. I did have a sort of McCartney-ish voice, a little rougher and higher. I sat in the studio with John and he played this old beat-up Gibson guitar and we just went through the song. He just kept playing it and singing the lead vocals very patiently while we worked out the background parts. And that was astonishing. It was me and John, the arranger, Jack, and the girl singers. The initial background part was a little too ambitious, so John made a suggestion to simplify it. We changed things on the spot. John worked out the parts with us. The girls couldn't stay in tune, so what happened was they started eliminating girls (laughs). We ended up singing, two girls and me, or maybe one girl and me. Then we layered some tracks that way. Then he dismissed the girls and I actually redid some of the girl's parts and then I did a couple of tracks where I was sort of shadowing some of John's leads. Jack always tells me, "I can hear you all over that track." I never heard the finished track until after he was killed. It's just a staggering song, it's so beautiful.

Jon Smith (assistant engineer, *Double Fantasy*): After John was killed I was up in the studio and I got a phone call from a deejay across the country somewhere. They were desperately trying to figure out what John says in the intro of the song, which was "For the other half of the sky." That was him saying, "This song is for Yoko."

Beautiful Boys

George Small (keyboards, *Double Fantasy*): That's a really interesting track. I think it's the most avant-garde track on the record because it has that flamenco, Spanish-flavored guitar solo, which Hughie played. The other thing I hear in that track are the backwards guitars. Of course, Lennon used that on "I'm Only Sleeping" from *Revolver*. It reminded me of one of the techniques that the Beatles used before.

Jon Smith (assistant engineer, *Double Fantasy*): Jack had an idea that we'd use the sound effects from a *Star Wars* battle scene going through the bridge of the song. At this point in the song Andy was playing time on his toms. We were going to send the battle sounds through noise gates, which keep the volume off until they get triggered to turn on by something else, which in this case were his toms. When a tom was hit, it would go (imitates beeping sci-fi sound effect noise). The sound effects would be timed to the drums. So we had a video machine and transferred the *Star Wars* audio onto tape and I was editing all of the dialogue out so we'd just have the battle sounds. The effect didn't make it to the final mix. When we finally had it working and we played it for Yoko, she didn't like it. She thought it was "too effect-y" and took away from the emotional mood of the song. We did use the battle sounds very low in the mix, but without gating them to the toms.

I happened to be on YouTube last year and I put in a search for "Lennon interview" and this amazing footage came up. It was taken with John and Yoko's camcorder—it's one of the first camcorders sold. This thing was huge; it was like a little attaché case with a long wire going to a camera that was also fairly large. They brought it to the studio a few times. Bob Gruen was there and he picked up the camera while John was doing an interview with the writer Robert Hilburn and just shot what was going on in the control room. John was being interviewed, Yoko was asleep on the couch in front of the console, and I was editing *Star Wars* sound effects. A lot of people online were wondering about the loud sound effects sounds you hear in the background. They couldn't figure out what we were doing. Some speculated that there was a film mix for a *Star Wars* film and that we were waiting to get into the room.

Dear Yoko

John Lennon: It's a nice track and it happens to be about my wife.[36]

Jack Douglas (producer, *Double Fantasy*): It had an early fifties feel to it that John was so good at because he was good at that rhythm. I thought it was the lightest, funniest track on the record.

George Small (keyboards, *Double Fantasy*): I just love that song.

It's such a fun song. That track kicks. Every time I hear that song it lifts me up. There's something great about the energy.

Tony Davilio (arranger, *Double Fantasy*): Hugh McCracken played four different harmonicas on "Dear Yoko." That gave it a unique sound.

Hugh McCracken (guitar, *Double Fantasy*): I play harmonica and slide guitar in unison on that song.

Earl Slick (guitar, *Double Fantasy*): Here's something that I'm not proud of . . . I was so fucking hungover and sick that day that I didn't show up at the studio. I called, but I didn't play on it. I was so fucked up that I couldn't get to the studio. This is part of who I was at the time. That was one of the very few times in all the years, even when I was out of control, that I ever did something like that and of course I did it on a Lennon record. (laughs)

Jack Douglas (producer, *Double Fantasy*): Because Earl wasn't there, that was Hughie's track in terms of how the guitars are structured. Hughie really took over the musical part of that song.

Every Man Has a Woman Who Loves Him

Tony Davilio (arranger, *Double Fantasy*): John jokingly called that song "Every Man Has a Wombat Who Loves Him." (laughs)

George Small (keyboards, *Double Fantasy*): That was the running joke for the song. It wasn't derogatory, it just made everybody laugh. It was because "woman" sounded like "wombat" and it was funny.

Earl Slick (guitar, *Double Fantasy*): That's a mellow tune. Guitar-wise, it was an easy, "play along with the guys" mellow track.

Jon Smith (assistant engineer, *Double Fantasy*): That's a Yoko song. John did a doubled harmony vocal all through it. I guess it was maybe 1982 where we decided to try and make a version with John's vocal being out front. We did it. It's kind of haunting because it wasn't meant to be a lead vocal. That came out years later on the *Milk and Honey* CD reissue.

Hard Times Are Over

Jon Smith (assistant engineer, *Double Fantasy*): We cut the track at the Hit Factory and it was a nice tune, but it didn't really come to life until we added the gospel choir.

Stan Vincent (Jack Douglas's business partner): John and Jack told me, "Get me a gospel black choir of thirty or forty people." I asked, "When do you want it?" and they'd go, "Tomorrow," and then I'd want to faint. They'd have these creative impulses and I was left with this giant task. I thought, How the hell do I get forty R&B gospel singers to a date the following day? But somehow I was able to get it done.

Julie Last (assistant engineer, *Double Fantasy*): We recorded a gospel choir [Kings Temple Choir] for the song "Hard Times Are Over" at A&R Studios.

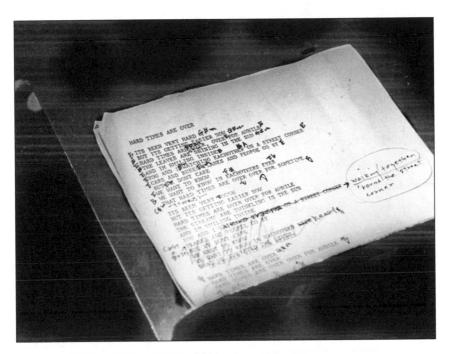

Lyrics for "Hard Times Are Over."

Jon Smith (assistant engineer, *Double Fantasy*): The room had these huge thirty, forty-foot ceilings and the sound was just great. We had this huge gospel choir in there and they'd be running down the parts and the sound just filled the room.

Julie Last (assistant engineer, *Double Fantasy*): It was done on a big soundstage and it was a large group, maybe twenty or thirty people standing on risers. The leader was sweet and respectful, the energy of the group pure and attentive. Yoko and John offered some guidance, then sat back and enjoyed the experience as the group really nailed the parts and the feeling.

Jack Douglas (producer, *Double Fantasy*): It was an incredible session, it was so spiritual.

Julie Last (assistant engineer, *Double Fantasy*): After the parts had been laid down, and the session was done, we started to stand up in the control room to get ready to leave when the leader of the choir said into the microphone, "Mr. Lennon, we have something we would like to give you." With that, he gave a signal and the choir started to sing. It was slow and achingly lovely. We all just listened in wonder. Then, at just the right moment, another signal, and the group kicked into a fast and riotously rousing spiritual. Nearly tore the roof off the place! Bodies swaying, hands clapping, voices rising in that way that makes you lift right off the ground. Everyone in that control room was beaming. What a great gift.

Jon Smith (assistant engineer, *Double Fantasy*): It was beautiful. It gave us all goose bumps. John and Yoko were very touched by it.

David Sheff (writer, *Playboy*): John and Yoko got incredibly emotional and had tears in their eyes.

Feeding Frenzy

Reports of John and Yoko's new album sent record companies into a feeding frenzy; all were on a mission to sign them to their label. Atlantic Records honcho Ahmet Ertegun breached security at the Hit Factory in an effort to make his pitch before being ejected from the studio. A new label, Geffen Records, which boasted a roster including Elton John and Donna Summer, would land the ultimate prize, John Lennon and Yoko Ono's *Double Fantasy*.

Tony Davilio (arranger, *Double Fantasy*): John and Yoko didn't have a record deal at the time they were working on *Double Fantasy* and they didn't want one because they wanted full control over the album. So if they paid for everything themselves, they'd have that control.

Earl Slick (guitar, *Double Fantasy*): When we went into the studio there was no label. Eventually they started talking about labels.

Howard Johnson (baritone sax, *Double Fantasy*): It had been six years since I last saw John when I played on *Walls and Bridges*. I asked him in the control room, "What label is this for?" He said, "Well, we don't know yet, we're gonna shop it." I said, "Shop it?! Don't you owe an album to Apple or EMI?" And he said, "No, I don't owe nobody any-thing. I own a hundred percent of my own ass for the first time since I was seventeen," and then he laughed. When we worked together before, he was going through a lot of problems. He was separated from Yoko, the government was trying to throw him out of the country because of this marijuana bust he had. He was out drinking every night with [Harry] Nilsson and Bobby Keys. Working with him on *Double Fantasy*, you could sense John was in a better state of mind because he was free.

Stan Vincent (Jack Douglas's business partner): John told me he wanted to beat Paul McCartney's record deal with Columbia. I don't think they ever beat that when they signed with Geffen. What Paul did was the usual; he made one deal with one company for the whole world. That's what most people do. I said to John and Yoko, "Let's license the record to the world, you'll get an advance and you'll own your master after the license term expires. Then we'll license it separately for the United States, Europe, Asia, and South America." Doing it that way, you wind up with a lot more money and you wind up owning your own master because the master rights would revert back to them after the licenses are up.

Jack Douglas (producer, *Double Fantasy*): I always thought that Stan Vincent, my business manager, should have made the deal. He would have gotten John exactly what he wanted. But they didn't want that kind of control going out of the house. It was gonna be done by Yoko. I was getting phone calls from people after it was announced the record was being done. Bruce Lundvall from Columbia called me and said, "We're prepared to offer John the exact deal Paul has."

Stan Vincent (Jack Douglas's business partner): I got a barrage of phone calls from many high-powered record company presidents.

One of them jokingly said they'd do unnatural acts with their sister in my living room if they could sign them (laughs). Once the word leaked that the album was being recorded, every record exec called me and I passed on all the relevant information to Yoko and John.

Lee DeCarlo (engineer, *Double Fantasy*): Stiff Records had a motto, "If it ain't Stiff, it ain't worth a fuck." The guy from Stiff Records sent John a telegram saying, "Heard you are recording. We're prepared to offer five thousand dollars to sign with us." John laughed and said, "Who the hell is Stiff Records?" and I told him. He said, "Jeez, that's funny."

Yoko Ono: All these record companies were coming after us because this was after five years of silence and John was coming back with an album. They realized this was very important for the music world so all the labels were coming. John was saying, "Listen, everybody knows that you are doing the business. They have to come to you, not me." They didn't want to come to me, of course. They were saying, "We don't want to go to the dragon lady. What is this?" (laughs) One big record company person called in when we were in the recording studio and said, "Ah, is John there, please?" I said, "Yes, it's Yoko, may I help you?" "No, no, I wanna talk to John." (laughs) They could be so rude. I'd go to John about this and he'd say, "Don't bother me with this. Just hang up on him." (laughs) I didn't actually hang up on him, but I said, "I'm sorry, but John is not available now." So that kind of stuff was going on.

One guy [Ahmet Ertegun] came upstairs to the studio and he was not allowed to enter. He was this big record company guy and he thought the studio would just let him in.

Jack Douglas (producer, *Double Fantasy*): Ahmet was on another floor with another artist. So he just said, "I'm gonna come up and see John and try and talk to him about a record deal." And he came up in the elevator, the elevator door opened, and there was John's security guy standing there. He didn't know who this big Turkish guy was (laughs). Ahmet said, "Do you know who I am?" And he said, "I don't care who you are, you can't come in." "But I'm Ahmet Ertegun!"

Yoko Ono: So I said to John, "Ahmet's here." John said, "No, no, no, just tell him he can't come in." (laughs) So Ahmet couldn't even come into the studio. John was saying, "If anybody does that, I don't wanna know, everybody has to come to you." But nobody was coming to me. And then I got a telegram from David Geffen. It said he wanted to talk to me about the record. I showed that telegram to John and he said, "That's the guy." You see, David's a very clever guy. He immediately knew that he had to get in touch with me, whether he liked that or not, I don't know. David didn't act like the president of a record company, he was like us.

Jack Douglas (producer, *Double Fantasy*): I knew David for a long time. John and Yoko said, "Do you know this guy? What do you think?" I thought that the way David got that deal was brilliant. He didn't give John the same deal as Paul [McCartney] was getting at Columbia because Geffen Records was just a start-up company. But he said something absolutely brilliant that got him the deal. "I'm not only getting one great artist, I'm getting two." Brilliant. And he absolutely believed it. The rest of the labels were only interested in John, and Yoko was a side thing.

David Geffen (Geffen Records): I had already signed Elton John and Donna Summer to my new label, but nothing had been released at that time.

Ed Rosenblatt (president, Geffen Records): I got a phone call from Phil Spector that John was in the studio with Jack [Douglas]. I asked David if he knew Yoko and he said he did and that he would send her a letter, which he did immediately.

David Geffen (Geffen Records): I wrote Yoko a letter and in the letter I indicated that I was interested in making a deal for that record and then forgot about it. I didn't think I was gonna get a response. I knew they lived at the Dakota so I sent it to the Dakota. I get a call and my secretary says, "Yoko Ono is on the phone." And I thought it's a joke. I got on the phone with her and I still thought it was a joke and then I realized it wasn't a joke. She said that she wanted me to come and talk to her in New York. So I flew into New York the next day and met with her. She asked me my address, my phone number, my birthday. She said she believed in numerology and said, "Are you worried?" And I said, "No." And she said, "Why not?" And I said, "Because my life is too good for my numbers not to be good." And they turned out to be good. I think Yoko probably told me what she wanted [one million dollars] and that she wanted the contract all on one page. And I agreed to all of that. But I told her it was in her best interest to have a long-form agreement, but I would do whatever she wanted. That's what she wanted and that's what we did. We made the deal after that one meeting. I met with John immediately after we made the deal. I hadn't heard the record until after I made the deal with them.

John Lennon: We decided to have made it first and answer all the letters and enquiries that came, you know, wanting to have the album . . . we eliminated the ones that said, Can we hear it first?[37]

Ed Rosenblatt (president, Geffen Records): With an artist like

John Lennon you didn't need to hear it ahead of time. These are people you want your label to be associated with.

David Geffen (Geffen Records): They played me three tracks and I thought they were all hits. I felt that John knew more about making hits than I did so I had no suggestions.

Tony Davilio (arranger, *Double Fantasy*): Sometime in September, I remember that Yoko walked in with a big smile on her face. She had on a very Oriental-looking black leather jacket with a multicolored dragon on the back of it. John asked her, "How many dragons did you slay today, Mother?" Then she told him the good news. Right after that, John excitedly called to me and said, "Tony, we just signed with Geffen Records!" At the time Geffen was a new label just starting out and John was their big signing.

Ed Rosenblatt (president, Geffen Records): It had been some time since John had put out a record so he hadn't sold a lot of records in that five-year break from music. But that was not important. It was important for us as a young record company to be associated with artists of the likes of Donna [Summer], Elton [John], and certainly John Lennon. That put us on the map. John Lennon was one of my idols and I loved everything he did, but to be able to be involved with someone like John Lennon on a professional standpoint was quite a thrill for a new record company label. This is what you get in the business for. If you looked at a list of a thousand artists, he's at the top. Later on I spoke with Yoko about why they signed with Geffen Records. I think she felt that David already had a lot of money so he was not out to just get rich with his new label. He was already rich so she felt comfortable with that.

Fantasy Becomes Reality

On November 17, 1980, *Double Fantasy* is released in America and Britain. The first single, "(Just Like) Starting Over," released on October 24, is an unqualified hit.

John Lennon: It's still a thrill to hear your record on the radio. It makes the music real to me even though I've heard the songs a million times in the studio. It also makes me feel good the way the disc jockeys are responding to it. When they play the song, the deejays don't have to say anything, but they've been all saying all sorts of wonderful things. That makes me feel that they really like it. Yoko and I are so excited that we're going right back into the studio to begin working on the next album. I feel just like a kid again.[38]

Bob Gruen (photographer and friend): At the end of October, they'd mixed "Starting Over" for release as a single and were mixing the rest of the album. John and Yoko were tipped off that WNEW, a New York radio station, was going to play "Starting Over" for the first time. So a bunch of us, including John and Yoko, went into this side room and listened to it being played on the radio on this mini-boom box.

Yoko Ono: Both of us were very happy that people liked the record. I remember when we heard it playing on the radio, we just sat around and listened. It was really great.

Bob Gruen (photographer and friend): They were very excited and listened closely, leaning over the boom box to hear what the deejay was saying and how the music sounded coming over the airwaves. John and Yoko danced around the room while the song played. Then the deejay came on and said he liked it so much he was gonna play it again. There was a brief moment where I think they felt a bit miffed because the album was the statement of a couple. They would have liked it if the deejay played Yoko's song, which was the B-side.

Paul Goresh (photographer): It was Tuesday, November 17, 1980. I remember it well because that was the day *Double Fantasy* was released. I was waiting at the Dakota to meet John to take photos of him in the park and he was running late. Finally he showed up and under his arm he was carrying four gray Warner/Elektra-Asylum envelopes. He'd been out late the night before and said he was sorry that we wouldn't be able to do what we planned. Then he said, "You know the album came out today, do you want one?" So he pulled one out for me and while he was doing it a guy came up and jumped in and said, "Can I get one, too?" And John looked at him and said, "Yeah, Sam Goody's on Forty-eighth Street has them." (laughs)

Dave Sholin (national music director and interviewer, RKO Radio): The album wasn't a slam dunk with radio. But when your name is John Lennon you're gonna get airplay and radio people are gonna listen to it right away. "Starting Over" was already a massive hit. That really raised the anticipation with the radio community. People were thinking, Wow, this is great, I wonder what the rest of the album is gonna sound like? No one was disappointed in the record. All the other singles, "Watching the Wheels" and "Woman," would have become hits anyway had John not been killed.

David Geffen (Geffen Records): When *Double Fantasy* was released, like all records, some people loved it and some people criticized it. John and Yoko believed in wishing. When John got killed I took Yoko home from the hospital. When I took Yoko into the apartment, on their door was the *Billboard* chart. Back then, they used to have the four-fold *Billboard* chart that was four times the size of the magazine. That week on the charts I think the record was at number nine with a bullet. On the chart John and Yoko had circled the record with an arrow to number one. And of course on the next *Billboard* chart it was number one.

Yoko Ono: The album and single didn't do well initially. Each time when we make something, like *Imagine*, we'd think it was gonna be number one and it was number two. It was like, Oh dear. Of course we wanted *Double Fantasy* to be number one. Then in England, the single, "Starting Over," only went to number eight. I went to John and said, "Listen, I'm sorry, John, it didn't make it. It's number eight." And he just looked at me, it was a very sort of silent but intense moment, and said, "Look, we have the family so don't worry about it."

Spreading the Gospel

Within Warner Bros. Records headquarters, excitement among the staff was high regarding their new high-profile artists.

Bert Keane (national promotion director, Warner Bros. Records): Geffen Records was a subsidiary label of ours. We'd worked with George Harrison and were familiar with superstars because we had a lot of them on the label. But this was *John Lennon*. Everybody at the label was all pumped up because he hadn't done a record in so long and the music was fabulous.

Bob Merlis (publicity director, Warner Bros. Records): It was a calling card for David Geffen to go out and sign John Lennon. It showed that David was serious about being in the big leagues, having already signed Elton John and Donna Summer to his new label. By signing Lennon you felt Geffen Records was a label to be reckoned with. David Geffen and Eddie Rosenblatt called the shots and we were the facilitators on their behalf because at that time they didn't have a very big staff. Eddie Rosenblatt and I went to visit Yoko to talk about the launch of the album and discuss the timetable of getting press materials and photos.

Ed Rosenblatt (president, Geffen Records): She had a great deal of input on how we should launch the album. She was very firm in what she wanted and very protective of John. She had a great understanding of John and his place in the history of popular music and wanted to make sure we didn't damage any of that.

Bob Merlis (publicity director, Warner Bros. Records): It was an event mentality in terms of making an impression on the press. It was more than just a record that you'd work. This was *John Lennon*. It was as close as you could come to the apogee of pop and rock. At the press level, they dealt with it as a serious John and Yoko album and were treated accordingly.

Ed Rosenblatt (president, Geffen Records): Retail was certainly open to the record. We had a good initial order. John had been away for quite a while. It was a different kind of record but it was a John and Yoko record with alternating tracks.

Bob Merlis (publicity director, Warner Bros. Records): *Double Fantasy* seemed like a very important work. The only qualm was it was a John and Yoko album; it wasn't a John Lennon album. John Lennon was a Beatle, Yoko was not. John Lennon had hit records on his own and Yoko did not. But she was thought of as a valid artist, especially in underground FM circles. It was an unusually configured album and that's the only thing that gave us cause for pause.

The initial response from radio was pretty good. It was John Lennon. You just needed to put the record out, make it available to radio, and just get out of the way.

In the Media

Five years out of the spotlight made John and Yoko a prized commodity with the international media. Once word spread about their impending new record, the record company was inundated with countless interview requests. Media savvy, John and Yoko carefully orchestrated their own press campaign, granting interviews to a select few major print outlets: *Newsweek*, *Playboy*, *Rolling Stone*, and the *Los Angeles Times*. John's all-encompassing conversation with *Playboy*'s David Sheff stands alongside his historic 1970 interview with *Rolling Stone* publisher Jann Wenner as the most comprehensive and revealing interview he ever gave.

David Sheff (writer, *Playboy*): I was given the assignment by an editor at *Playboy*, sort of an offhanded remark, "Any chance you can get to John and Yoko?" I had no idea if I could, but said I would try. I ended up firing off hundreds of letters to all kinds of people. One day I got a phone call from one of Yoko's assistants asking when I was born, where I was born, those kinds of things. Based on my astrological charts and numerological numbers Yoko wanted to meet me. I flew to New York and met with her. Based on that meeting she said, "Let's go forward." It was all luck and timing and things that were way beyond my control. They were already at work on *Double Fantasy*. They'd made the decision they were gonna do two print interviews, one for a weekly and one for a monthly. Only now almost thirty years later do I know how remarkable that interview was. I've done hundreds of interviews since then, but at that time I had not done that many. So the idea of spending three weeks, day in and day out with anyone of the stature of John Lennon—especially with John Lennon *and* Yoko Ono—was unprecedented. I was with them while they were making *Double Fantasy*. Every day I'd meet them at the Dakota. Oftentimes during the course of a day we'd only talk for an hour or two, but I spent all that time in the studio watching them record so many of those songs.

I watched them record almost all of "Starting Over." That was so exciting. They knew it would be the song that would start the record. It was a statement relating to them starting over in their lives and the song represented that.

I remember everything about the recording of "Woman," from beginning to end, and watching how the track, which meant so much to John, came into shape and how they'd change things as it went along. Sometimes John would get inspired to try something different and that was exciting to see. I remember sitting there with John, listening to other people put down their tracks and then John putting on his lead vocals and guitar tracks. There would be times that I'd be in the Hit Factory and I'd be in one room with one of them while the other would be laying down a track. Sometimes John would sit and dreamily stop talking for a minute to listen to what was going on in the other room.

One day I remember John greeted me at the Dakota by singing the words to "Eleanor Rigby" redone as "Here's David Sheff, come to ask questions with answers that no one would hear."

John was so open and devoted to being honest to the point that it was startling sometimes how committed he was to those ideals. I'd often get lost in the conversation. He was talking about the kind of things that I would think about, how to conduct my life and be a better person. Because he was so warm, open, and gracious, I would forget who I was talking to. Then all of a sudden he would make a reference and say, "And that's when I wrote 'Strawberry Fields'" and I'd realize, Oh my God, this is John Lennon! I've talked to people who will never allow you for a minute to forget that they are the pop star or the movie star or the politician or the writer. It's so much about who they are that they carry this defensiveness about it and they're trying to impress you all of the time. There was none of that with Lennon.

Here was John Lennon, who had accomplished as much as any artist could hope to accomplish, and yet what was his message? The part of John's message about his love for Yoko, what had given him sustenance and what had given him grounding after a life of ups and downs and struggles, none of that contentment could be faked. I don't think I've ever been with two people who were more devoted to each other, more in love, more obsessed and infatuated with each other. I was really struck by that. Being the biggest pop star in the world had never given him the satisfaction and contentment that he found in this later stage of his life, which was devoted to being a father and being a husband. It's what *Double Fantasy* is all about and it's also reflected in him as a person. As an interviewer I know if you go and sit with somebody for an hour or two over lunch at the Four Seasons restaurant, which I've done, they can present anything they want to me. But when you spend three weeks with someone, from morning to night, you truly see who they are as a person. I saw that John was everything that he presented to the public. There was no pretense or attempt to try and create an image. There was no message he was trying to create that was different from who he was. It was one hundred percent genuine. I saw John and Yoko at their weak moments in the middle of the night when they were exhausted. I saw them when they were excited and I saw them when they were frustrated that something wasn't working right.

My editor [Barry Golson] and I thought that our piece would mark the first time John and Yoko were coming out to talk to the public. I don't know if it was promised just to *Playboy*, maybe it was *Newsweek*, too, but if that was gonna be true our understanding was they were both gonna come out at the same time. What happened was *Newsweek* came out before *Playboy* and I got a call from my editor. We went over to the Dakota and met with John and Yoko. My editor said, "Hey, wait a second, we had an exclusive, what's going on here?" Rather than being defensive about it or apologetic, John said, "What can we do to make it up to you guys?" My editor brilliantly said, "Let's do something no one has ever done before, let's tell the story behind every Beatles song." And John said, "Great, let's do it." The idea of looking at the Beatles songs was exciting to him. He said, "I'm proud of my work with the Beatles and I'd be happy to talk about that forever." Because it was too noisy in Yoko's office, for much of that interview we sat on the marble floor in this big white bathroom. It was an amazing experience to hear him speak about the songs he wrote or co-wrote with Paul [McCartney]. The one album that affected me more than any other album is John Lennon's *Plastic Ono Band* record and the song "God." "Strawberry Fields Forever" is the one song of John's that defined my childhood. Because of that feeling to me when that song came up, it led into so many amazing stories. He explained the song line by line. Because of the moment and my interest, he dove into certain songs in ways that were so extraordinary. It would have been lovely to have had the opportunity to do that with every song that he ever wrote.

• • •

While most artists embark on a media blitz upon the release of a new album, John and Yoko only granted a few interviews to promote Double Fantasy.

Bert Keane (national promotion director, Warner Bros. Records): John and Yoko didn't do many interviews to promote the record. We worked the album on the strength of Lennon and the sound of the record. It was like dealing with [Frank] Sinatra. Sinatra didn't do interviews. When you're dealing with an artist that has those dictates, you just have to go with their music. And in this case, the music was enough to sell the record. The album was doing very well and it was just starting to build. The momentum was going off the strength of "Starting Over." We were starting to get a lot of FM airplay and that's really how you sold albums. Radio was also starting to dig into "Watching the Wheels."

Dave Sholin (national music director and interviewer, RKO Radio): It was the fall of 1980, I was in L.A. and I spent some time with David Geffen. He called and said, "I have something I want to play for you." So I went to his office on Sunset Boulevard. We sat down and he played "Starting Over" without telling me who it was. I had no idea. None. I thought, it sounds like someone's trying to do an Elvis kind of thing. It had an Elvis vibe. I later found out when I interviewed John that the Elvis vibe was intentional. So I said to David Geffen, "Who is this?" Then he told me who it was. I thought it was phenomenal. Before John dropped out of music for five years to raise Sean, we hadn't heard much about what he was doing. So hearing "Starting Over" for the first time was amazing. David told me, "We're granting one radio interview for America and we'd like you to conduct it." He asked me if I wanted to do it and it took me about a nano second to say yes. I'd interviewed Paul [McCartney] and Linda [McCartney] in London in 1979 for the *Back to the Egg* album. It's kind of unbelievable that a year later I got the chance to interview John and Yoko.

Sound Off

When released back in November 1980, *Double Fantasy* polarized music reviewers; some hailed it as a welcome return to form, while others derided John's songs as being soft and "safe as milk" and championed Yoko's more adventurous and avant-garde material.

John Swenson (music writer, *Creem* magazine): John had been on the sidelines for five years. He was still an icon and a leader of a generation, both politically and aesthetically. People still looked up to him. Everybody hung on to any glimmer of information about what he was doing during this time. Then we heard he and Yoko were making this record together. There was interest from the press about the new record and also a certain amount of cynicism, too. Some of the catty Hollywood gossip columns focused on him being a house husband and questioned why he stopped making music in the first place. John and Yoko were very polarizing figures. They were definitely ahead of their time, but the wise guy pundits never liked them because they weren't playing the media stardom game or they were playing it for their own purposes.

I heard the record before John was killed and reviewed it for

Creem. My review was definitely positive. Lennon has changed from being an ex-Beatle to being Yoko's partner. Their ability to make a record together was a real step forward conceptually and it meant that there was probably a lot more of interest to be heard from John Lennon in the future. The contrast back and forth between John and Yoko's songs was unique. They were placed one after the other and shared a certain rhythm-and-response quality to it, which really interested me. I thought that worked really well. I liked some of the songs better than others. "Watching the Wheels" and "Starting Over" really stood out.

I do remember thinking that the album wasn't the next logical step after his last solo record (*Walls and Bridges*). Yoko's music was always more experimental. History has proven that Yoko was an avant-garde forward-looking stylist who was influential a generation later.

Double Fantasy wasn't John's best record, but it was a different direction. This record was an indication of where they were going together on a creative level. They were certainly a great New York love story.

Bill King (music writer, *Atlanta Constitution*): I was the rock critic for the *Atlanta Constitution* and reviewed *Double Fantasy* when it came out. I felt it was really only half a Lennon album. The songs alternated to form a male-female dialogue focusing on their relationship over the past few years, which I thought made for an interesting exchange of ideas and emotions. Unfortunately, it didn't make for the most pleasant listening experience. It was true that new wave caught up with Yoko's early seventies avant-garde recordings and it was also true that the songs she recorded for *Double Fantasy* are the most accessible of her career, but that's all relative. I did think "Kiss Kiss Kiss" was her most successful cut. Despite these songs being her most accessible tunes, she was still nowhere near in John Lennon's league as a songwriter or singer.

As a result of the alternating cuts, this was in the LP days, you couldn't listen to John's new recordings in five years without lifting the needle, which made *Double Fantasy* a frustrating album, especially since John's own songs were delightful. I remember I said that those who were expecting John to sound like Talking Heads were gonna be disappointed. This wasn't the same composer of anguished rejections of his Beatles past in "God." This was a John Lennon who wrote about the comforts of home, marital love, and fatherhood. I wrote that it sounded like Paul McCartney's musical turf.

Stephen Pond of the *L.A. Times* dismissed Lennon as sounding like an aging hippie on the album, but to me Lennon handled those themes with a minimum of cloying sentiment and a great deal of honest, exhilarating emotion.

I liked the single, "Starting Over" and had grown to like "Beautiful Boy." It took some time to grow on me as I initially thought it was a little soft. I also liked "Watching the Wheels." The album wasn't all sweetness and light. Much of Yoko's material carried a bite reminiscent of the 1970-ish Lennon, particularly "Give Me Something" and "I'm Moving On." "I'm Losing You" featured a really nice guitar hook and addresses the communication problems that sometimes spring up in the best marriages. But for my money, the best thing on the album and the song of the year was "Woman." It had a haunting melody, which built very effectively and lyrics in which Lennon admitted he was responsible for some of the couple's past problems. There was a vulnerability in his voice when he sang, "My life is in your hands."

Jon Young (music writer, *Trouser Press*): I got an assignment from *Trouser Press* to review *Double Fantasy* because I'd done a long overview piece of Lennon's career when he was silent. Everybody was glad to hear from him again. There was a lot of anticipation about the record. My opinion about the album has changed over the years. At the time I liked it and enjoyed John's ballads, but I think he seemed rusty. I remember pulling my punches. I was probably nicer than I wanted to be just because it was great to hear him again. I was not one of those people who disliked Yoko. I always tried to cut her some slack, but I wasn't really interested in her music and didn't pay much attention to Yoko's songs.

In retrospect I think it's a much weaker album than it seemed at the time, but it was just good to have any new John Lennon music because no one knew if he would ever record again. Lennon was always writing about his own life, that's where he was at the time, enjoying the pleasures of home. It's kind of tame stuff now, but you can't discount it. So I remember liking the album, but it didn't stick with me much. If he hadn't been killed, I'm sure it would have been filed away even quicker. I think he probably would have gone on to do more interesting music.

Robert Christgau (music writer, *Village Voice*): At the time, I was hoping that Lennon, who was a real hero for many of us, would respond to the same aesthetic imperatives which we were responding to. This had to do with a rougher, more primitive kind of rock and roll made in a band format rather than well-played, carefully produced studio rock. I am less inclined to be puritanical or monolithic in what I demand of an artist. I'm not inclined to dismiss something out of hand because the approach seems wrong. That isn't to say there wasn't a certain unease with the sound of the record on my part. But without any question, that unease was blown away by his murder.

I always liked John's lyrics on the record. I was already a happily married man who regarded the writing of good songs about domestic love, conjugal love, as a demonstrably difficult but extremely worthwhile thing to do. There wasn't any question in my mind that as an aesthetic project I thought this was a good thing to do. It wasn't what most rockers thought was an appropriate subject matter for rock and roll. I thought John succeeded in making credible pop music about a happy marriage. I've seen many people try to do that and fail. In general, conflict is easier to make art out of than tranquility.

I thought Yoko's songs on *Double Fantasy* were fine. I've always been sympathetic to Yoko's art. I don't like the art that now has a fan base, which is avant-garde, minimalist stuff. But I liked a lot of her conceptual stuff. I liked *Grapefruit* and wrote a famous piece about it called "Like a Horse and Carriage." John and Yoko liked that piece so much that they actually called me up and flew me to Syracuse to see her show.

I think *Double Fantasy* is a very successful record and I also think *Milk and Honey* is a very successful record; I like it almost as much as I like *Double Fantasy*.

I don't usually fluctuate wildly with what I initially thought about an album because I wait until I know what I think. That's part of my method. My judgment is very solid and sure. But records do tend to either gain or lose aura as decades pass. I would say *Double Fantasy* is one of the many excellent records that has gained a certain aura, glow, stature, and presence. It is a record I do occasionally play. For me to say I play anybody is a big deal because I still spend sixty to seventy hours a week listening to new music. I don't have the time to revisit records much, but John Lennon is somebody who I do revisit because I care about him.

Charles Shaar Murray (music writer, *NME*): I reviewed the album for *NME*. I felt John's songs were complacent and solipsistic at a time when the best rock music of the previous few years had been intimately concerned with the world outside, which was engaged with the environment and the zeitgeist in a way that Lennon himself had been at the start of the decade. Remember, this was punk time. Punk was still alive. *Double Fantasy* came out within a year of things like *London Calling* [the Clash] and the first Gang of Four album.

When I wrote that review I was young and intolerant and full of drugs. I didn't appreciate at the time what being forty and a parent meant. Lennon had been making music all his life until the mid-seventies. After having been through that whole faintly ludicrous high politics phase where he was basically induced into making a fool of himself by the Jerry Rubins of this world, he was tired and wanted to take a break to regroup and reassess. When you're in your twenties operating at a very high energy level, thanks to both natural and unnatural energy and the whole punk rock explosion is happening around you, the kind of thing that Lennon was trying to do on that album is not going to impress you that much. We wanted the fighting, high-energy John, and the punk spirit of the Beatles 'cause in the Beatles Lennon was the resident punk. The stuff on the *Plastic Ono Band* album was very introspective, but it had a raw, harsh edge, which appealed to me. In the sky of my music, my two major guiding stars that I follow are a blues star and a punk star. The *Plastic Ono Band* album and the "Cold Turkey" single, in its raw, first-person honesty, appealed to my blues buds and my punk buds. I felt let down by Lennon's songs on *Double Fantasy*.

But the thing is I wasn't a parent then and I'm still in a child-free zone at my current advanced age. Phil Lynott of Thin Lizzy had written a song about his baby daughter and I was going, "It's not fuckin' rock and roll to be writing songs about your fuckin' kids!" And I felt the same way about John with a song like "Beautiful Boy."

As a grown-up I can now totally appreciate the emotion that led him to write that song. But back then what I wanted was for Lennon to come back rockin' and make common cause with the punks and he did the exact opposite of that. I thought Yoko's songs on that album had an edge that his stuff didn't. I thought she was still experimenting and going for stuff. I thought Lennon was being musically very lazy. But sometimes an artist wants to create within their comfort zone. As a man approaching sixty, I now understand this. Back then as a man approaching thirty, I didn't.

Around the *NME* office, I remember when the "Starting Over" single came out, we all liked it. We thought that really rocked and had a good vibe to it. But I think none of us around the office liked Lennon's songs on that album very much. But none of that diminished our horror and anguish at his assassination. I was thinking, I couldn't give a fuck if he just made a record I didn't like, I wanted him to live long and prosper. The idea of a world without John Lennon was horrifying to me and still is. That was absolutely nightmarish. For me, in the flattening out of time that you get with memory, it seemed like one second I was putting down his comeback album and the next I was writing his fuckin' obituary.

(*Author's note: Charles Shaar Murray wrote this retrospective reassessment of the album twenty years later in a review that appeared in the October edition of* Mojo *magazine.*)

Double Fantasy *brings Lennon back into the arena after his "lost weekend" and his house-husband sabbatical. Your humble servant canned the album in the* NME *when it was released in the punk-fallout era: after all, we'd been giving*

Macca a hard time all decade for his twee paeans to bour-geois domesticity, so at least we were even-handed. Never-theless, when the album's lead-off single, "Starting Over," arrived, the mere sound of Lennon's voice—slapback and all—had raised a spontaneous cheer in the office.

Cut with a monstrous regiment of En Why session-maf musos, the core players being Earl Slick and Hugh Mc-Cracken on guitars, Tony Levin on bass, and Andy Newmark on drums, it was sharp-end-of-the-mainstream studio rock in which Lennon's songs—the edgiest of which were "Cleanup Time" and the twitchy "I'm Losing You"—are eclipsed by the parallel performances by Yoko with which they alternate. Framed by the rock-solid pop (or, if you prefer, the pop-friendly rock) of the settings Lennon and his crew concoct for her, she sounds like Bjork's godmother on the likes of "Kiss Kiss Kiss," "I'm Moving On" and, most powerfully of all, on the added-on "Walking on Thin Ice," begun before, but com-pleted after, Lennon's death. If Plastic Ono Band is essential to our understanding of Lennon's life and art, then the Ono songs on Double Fantasy represent the most direct route into Yoko's.

What a difference two decades makes: the time which has passed since Lennon's assassination. The retro-Britpop sensi-bility which has dominated most of the past decade's worth of local-white-boys-with-guitars means, effectively, that this music—cut when the personnel of said bands were infants or unborn—speaks with an eerie immediacy which few deceased rockers this side of Hendrix could match.

Johnny O'Boogie—wish you were here.

Touring

Reenergized by the *Double Fantasy* recording sessions, Lennon was musically reborn and planning to embark on his first solo tour.

Hugh McCracken (guitar, *Double Fantasy*): In the beginning there was no talk of touring. But as the project neared completion, that changed.

John Lennon: I'm so hungry for making records because of the way I feel. I want to make some more records before I tour, so I'd like to make at least one more album before actually making that final decision of calling those very expensive session musicians and taking them on the road. When I went in I had no intention of going live because I noticed a lot of people like the Clash don't do any personal appearances anymore. They just make a video and a record. We were playing in the studio and then I don't know whether it was Tony, the bass player, or the drummer after we'd done "Starting Over." He said, "Can we do this again? I mean, let's take it on the road." And that was the first time it came out. And I thought, My God, this would be fun, wouldn't it? And if we could do it in the way we've done the album, which is have fun, enjoy the music, enjoy the performance, be accepted as John and Yoko, then I'd be happy to go out there . . . It's certainly a very big possibility when we get the next album tucked away and people know the songs from *Double Fantasy*, we can go out and perform from *Double Fantasy* and the new album rather than having to go back to "Imagine," although we might do it, or even before "Imagine." I don't really wanna go out and do (sings) "Yesterday, all my troubles seemed so far away . . ." (laughs)[39]

Jack Douglas (producer, *Double Fantasy*): He was gonna do Beatle songs and was talking to the band about how he wanted to rearrange them and make them really contemporary, songs like "I Want to Hold Your Hand" and "She Loves You."

Yoko Ono: We were gonna tour behind *Double Fantasy*. John was so John. He was saying, "I wanna do 'I Want to Hold Your Hand' because that was mine, we did it in the Beatles, but it was mine. You're gonna do all of your wailing and all that. You're gonna show them it's not old hat. We're gonna do 'I Want to Hold Your Hand' and your freak stuff." Then he said, "I'm gonna sing 'I Want to Hold Your Hand' and I'm just gonna kneel in front of everybody and hold your hand, okay?" (laughs) I was saying, "John, this is not gonna work. Nobody's gonna come." (laughs) When the B-52s did it [paying homage to Yoko's music and vocal style], it was fine. They're a great group and people could accept it. But not with me. They'd say, "C'mon, she's the dragon lady." At the time, people were not gonna accept it. That's exactly how it was. When John said, "Your time has come, we're gonna go on tour and you're gonna do your stuff," he didn't realize my music would not have been received well.

Howard Johnson (baritone sax, *Double Fantasy*): I came to the horn session for the *Double Fantasy* album from a rehearsal with Paul Simon. I was part of his touring band for the album *One Trick Pony*. John wanted to get some inside information about how Paul's tour was being set up. At the same time, John and I talked about me putting together a horn section together for a tour to support *Double Fantasy*. So he asked me about Paul's show. I said, "It's a one-hour set, a fifteen minute break, and than another one-hour set." And he said, "Simon's doing two hours?" I said, "Yeah, that's kind of standard." He said, "Really? We'd just do a single forty-minute set!" And I said, "Forty minutes? That shit went out with the Beatles!" And the people in the control room were aghast that I spoke to him like that, but it was okay because John and I laughed.

Andy Newmark (drummer, *Double Fantasy*): I recall that John wanted to go out and play. He indicated that from time to time in the studio, just casually. I was really glad to hear him being that enthusiastic and I was thrilled at the idea of playing live shows with him. He'd go, "Yeah, this'll be good live. I want to play this stuff in front of people." My feeling is that John would have definitely performed live in that following year, 1981. He had enough tracks recorded and almost completed for the follow-up record, I recall his plan was to release *Milk and Honey* quite soon after *Double Fantasy* and then go out and play some concerts. Had he eventually gone out and performed, I am sure it would have been with this band, these musicians making *Double Fantasy*, including myself. Sadly, we never got to do that with John.

Earl Slick (guitar, *Double Fantasy*): On the last day of the session John asked me what my schedule was. At the time I was signed with Columbia and had an album to do and a tour. I said, "I'm under contract and I have to get this record done." He said, "Do the record, but what about touring?" He loved the band and said, "I want to go out and do dates in major markets." I said, "Of course I want to do it." He said, "What if I just called up Columbia and took care of it?" And I said, "Fine, I'm in." If John Lennon called them up and said he was gonna take me on tour, they weren't gonna have a problem with it (laughs).

Stan Vincent (Jack Douglas's business partner): We were at Mr. Chow's on East Fifty-seventh Street and we're all sitting at this very long table. The band was there and I was sitting next to John. We had a great dinner, lots of laughing. I turned to John and said, "Listen, look what you've just finished. You've got to go on the road with this band and play live." He said, "No, I don't wanna go on tour." I kept on him and he said, "All right, I only want to do one night in major cities." I had my martini in front of me and said, "Are you gonna do it?" And he said, "Yeah, yeah yeah . . ." in this kind of wanting to do it but disgruntled way. I got up in front of the musicians, held my martini glass up, and said, "Gentlemen, we're going on tour!" And everybody rose up, saluted, and clinked glasses.

Hugh McCracken (guitar, *Double Fantasy*): At Mr. Chow's, it was made official with a toast that the tour was a go.

George Small (keyboards, *Double Fantasy*): My understanding was we were gonna do a world tour starting in Japan in March of 1981.

Bob Gruen (photographer and friend): In March he was gonna rehearse with the band and in April he was gonna go out on the road on a world tour. We talked about where we were gonna shop in

Tokyo and how we were gonna go to a store called "Milk Boy." We talked about where we were gonna eat in Paris. He was particularly excited about going back to play in England.

Jack Douglas (producer, *Double Fantasy*): John sketched up the stage production. His idea was the stage looked like either a spaceship or a crab depending on what your view was. It was saucerlike and it had two crablike arms that came out and on the arms were cameras and the cameras moved around. These cameras were gonna be like these others characters because of the way this claw moved around. There was gonna be a giant screen projecting all of this.

Lee DeCarlo (engineer, *Double Fantasy*): He had really futuristic ideas about touring. One idea was using holograms of the band onstage like *Star Trek*. They wouldn't actually be there; there'd be holograms of them onstage. Another was some kind of pay-per-view thing, playing live in one place and having it broadcast in theaters.

Tony Davilio (arranger, *Double Fantasy*): Yoko was really into astrology and she was regularly seeing an astrologist. One day I was in the little room across the studio, which had a tape recorder in there. They'd make me copies of the tracks and I'd be in there working on stuff with one of John's guitars, a cherry red Epiphone. She had her bag in there and I got up to get a cigarette and looked over and saw a piece of paper hanging out of it. Written in dark black ink, it said, "No tour now, danger around John." This was a warning she wrote down after seeing her astrologist.

The Final Sessions—
Walking on Thin Ice

Buoyed by the commercial success of the new album, December 1 found John and Yoko hunkered down for a weeklong session at the Record Plant, where they'd put the finishing touches on a promising new Yoko Ono dance track entitled "Walking on Thin Ice" and did a three-hour extensive interview with British disc jockey Andy Peebles of BBC Radio One.

Steve Marcantonio (engineer, "Walking on Thin Ice" session): We worked on the song from a Monday to a Monday [December 1–December 8]. They came in with the track "Walking on Thin Ice." We spent a few hours listening to it. As far as I remember, we took the bass and drums and maybe a guitar or two and then overdubbed everything. John added a spooky, haunting synth. He also played an incredible and amazing haunting guitar solo. Every time thereafter when it played back in the studio John and I would face each other and play air guitar. It was probably the most amazing experience I've ever had in the studio. The vibe was incredible. John and Yoko were in good spirits. A gentleman from the BBC [Andy Peebles] was there, doing an interview, and after they were done

John said, "Hang out." John was in a really good space and Yoko was really comfortable. He was very supportive of Yoko and called her "Mother" all of the time.

Jon Smith (assistant engineer, *Double Fantasy*): Even in its basic form "Walking on Thin Ice" was an amazing song. When we cut the track for it, it was electrifying. While the last note was ringing out on the master take, John hit the talkback and said, "Congratulations, Yoko, you've just cut your first number one single." We never did any overdubs on it at the Hit Factory, we just recorded the basic track, but we knew it was something special.

Bob Gruen (photographer and friend): John wanted to rush out "Walking on Thin Ice" in between *Double Fantasy* and the next record to capitalize on the fact that people were finally accepting Yoko's music. It was the first time she wasn't being vilified. He thought this new song of hers was great and wanted to get it out as soon as possible.

Yoko Ono: John's guitar playing on that song is great. Nobody can play like that. John was always saying, "Nobody notices my guitar playing," but he just blossomed. The avant-garde thing that I did, that's where he could do that kind of wild guitar playing.

Jon Smith (assistant engineer, *Double Fantasy*): John had added all these wild, screaming guitar parts to it and Yoko's vocals were fantastic. He couldn't wait until it was released and everyone would see what a great song Yoko had written and recorded. He was so proud of her, he was practically bursting.

Jack Douglas (producer, *Double Fantasy*): When we did

"Walking on Thin Ice," John said to me, "You know, this is the one that's gonna get Yoko really off the ground. She's gonna get the critics on her side, everybody." He said, "So the next record will be the boys only, if you know what I mean."

Bob Gruen (photographer and friend): The last time I saw John was early in the morning on December 6, sitting on the floor of the Record Plant studio in the doorway. John told me he was very excited that the album was receiving such good reviews, and most excited that Yoko was getting good reviews. John was a big fan of Yoko. He wasn't sorry that reviewers said Yoko's songs were more avant-garde, modern, and interesting than John's songs, which they described as being more MOR, middle of the road. And he said, "That's fine because we're going right down the middle of the road to the bank." (laughs)

James Ball (assistant mix engineer, *Double Fantasy*): While they were working on "Walking on Thin Ice," John and Yoko knew I was working in the studio downstairs and sent down a signed copy of *Double Fantasy*, which was inscribed "To James: have a ball." Out of the hundreds of artists I've worked with, they were the only ones who ever did that. That showed what classy people they were.

Jon Smith (assistant engineer, *Double Fantasy*): On December 6, John and Yoko had an interview scheduled with Andy Peebles of the BBC at the Hit Factory. Eddie Germano called and told me I was going to engineer it.

Andy Peebles (disc jockey, BBC Radio One): Bill Fowler, head of promotion for Warner Brothers in England, phoned up our office and said, "If I could get an interview with Lennon, would you be interested?" I said, "That's a pretty stupid question, Bill, of course I'd be interested, but I think your chances of getting it are pretty slim." He said he was confident he could make it happen. A week later he got back to me and told us it was on. Derek Chinnery, controller of Radio One, sanctioned we could go, but on one condition: in addition to the Lennon interview, we'd have to line up additional work to get the most value for our money, so we negotiated to talk to David Bowie, who at the time was appearing on Broadway in *The Elephant Man.*

So our team flew over to New York. Then we got a call from Yoko, who said we had to come to the Dakota to have an official meeting so she could decide whether or not she would give us the interview. We arrived at the Dakota, which was thrilling because I knew that Lauren Bacall and Roberta Flack and various luminaries of the entertainment industry had or were living there. We were taken into Yoko's office and she said, "I want you to tell me why we should give you this interview." She felt this was a decision that needed analyzing as they'd had offers from other radio stations like Capital Radio and Radio Luxembourg. After about twenty-five minutes of debate and discussion, she agreed that they would do the interview with the BBC. We asked if there was any chance of seeing John and she said, "No, he's upstairs looking after Sean, but we'll see you tomorrow at the Hit Factory at midday." So the next day I'm very wound up and have got butterflies. I've had thirty-five years in broadcasting, but this was the biggest interview I'd ever done for the simple reason that the man I was about to talk to was one of my great heroes. I'm fifty-nine years old and I grew up in an era when everybody formed pop groups and we did at school. Not only did I never dream that I would meet John, but I also never dreamt that I would sit with him later that night after the interview in Mr.

Chow's restaurant and he's asking me which Beatles songs my group played and how good were the band members. I was about to say to him, "Look, you've been really nice, but this isn't necessary" until it dawned on me very quickly that he actually was genuinely interested. He was fascinated that the Beatles had the power to have so many people around the world emulate what they'd done.

So we rolled up at the Hit Factory and they told us they'd just received a phone call from the Lennons, who asked if we could come back at six o'clock. I suppose I'm a pessimist by nature and I said to Paul Williams and Doreen Davis, who were my two BBC producers, "This isn't gonna happen." So we then had the longest six hours of my professional life, wandering up and down the streets of New York City doing a little Christmas shopping. We got back to the studio at ten to six and they were there.

John greeted me like a long-lost friend. It was quite extraordinary. I think the reason he was so great with us was because of the BBC. Yoko said to me that he listened a lot to the BBC World Service and every time Liverpool was mentioned he would get very tearful and homesick and start frantically reminiscing. During my interview, you could tell John was dreadfully homesick and would love to have gone back to Liverpool. He hadn't been home for ten years. He promised me he was gonna come to Britain and play concerts. He told me he wanted to sail up the Thames in a boat and arrive outside the House of Parliament and then he said he would come and do my show. He said, "I mean it, I'll bring my guitar." I believe had he lived he would have done that as I feel we struck up a very good rapport.

Jon Smith (assistant engineer, *Double Fantasy*): I set up a table and put three mics on it, one for John, one for Yoko, and one for

Andy. When they arrived John was jumping up and down, holding a cassette in his hand. He was so excited because they'd been doing overdubs on "Walking on Thin Ice" and he'd brought a copy to play for me. "You have to hear what we've done to this, put it on right away!"

Andy Peebles (disc jockey, BBC Radio One): That's the reason why John and Yoko were late to bed and asked us to come at six o'clock. They were working on mixing that song. John played it for me and asked, "What do you think?" I really liked it and thought it was a very clever piece of work, given that he'd done a lot of research at what was being played in the clubs. He was doing it as a love project for Yoko. I found the pair of them genuinely in love with each other. If that wasn't true they should have both been given a pair of Oscars to put on the mantelpiece. My feeling is that in their relationship there was a constant artistic battle. But the battle came from Yoko, who was desperate to be accepted and appreciated from everybody and she'd struggled to find it.

When we started the interview, it became apparent even to Yoko that this was gonna be John's interview and that she was gonna play a secondary role. I think she accepted that for the best of reasons and because of that, it made her involvement in the conversations a lot easier from my point of view. She occasionally interjected and said, "I never knew that" or "That's fascinating, you never told me that." There was such an outpouring of memories, facts, and stories from John that I was learning things I never knew. Certainly when John was talking about the early days of the Beatles that would have been fascinating to her because I'm sure there's a lot he never talked to her about. We were told by Yoko in our meeting that we'd get one hour for the interview. We talked for three hours and that was entirely down to John. So we must have gotten something right.

There's no way on God's earth that I would have talked to someone that long unless I wanted to.

John was exactly as I expected him to be. I was finally having a conversation with the guy that I'd seen interviewed endlessly over the years, from the days of him being the group comedian—"Those of you in the boxes, rattle your jewelry"—at the London Palladium, lines like that. We all knew how witty he was. We had an astounding interview and I was absolutely thrilled.

During the interview they'd sent out for food and it literally went cold on the table in the Hit Factory. When we took a break he told me he was starving. He asked one of the people who worked for them, "Can you phone and book a table at Mr. Chow's?" He said, "Let's all go for dinner after this because I'm really enjoying myself." When the interview finished the Lennons had two limousines outside and remarkably, and I was very touched by this, Yoko said, "You go with John to the restaurant" and the rest of the gang went into the other limo. We walked in the restaurant and came to the top of a staircase, which comes down into the restaurant. John was wearing a silver jacket with fox fur trim and a pair of dark glasses. I have to admit, I was enjoying the fact that I've just walked into one of New York's top restaurants with John Lennon. And what happened next really sums up John's humor. As we stood at the top of the staircase and the maître d' almost started to run up the stairs, John looked down and saw everyone in the restaurant looking up because they'd realized who'd just arrived. In that wonderful Liverpool voice he said, "Look at this, our Andrew, look at these people down there, they're all going, 'Who the fuck's that with Andy Peebles?'" (laughs) That was an old Jimmy Tarbuck line, who was the big comedian to come out of Liverpool at exactly the same time as the Beatles.

I remember spending most of the first five minutes at the table telling him "No Reply" was one of the best vocals he'd ever done.

He said, "Why do you think that?" I told him it was a wonderful song that was passionate and heartfelt. We spent another three hours at dinner.

Steve Marcantonio (engineer, "Walking on Thin Ice" session): We started mixing "Walking on Thin Ice" on Saturday or early Sunday. Late Sunday night, early Monday morning, we were burning the candle at both ends, all in a very clean manner. All we were doing was drinking coffee and eating food. Around three in the morning we were close to getting a mix. We were just gonna leave it set up and come back on Monday and listen to it. I needed a break and needed to get outside. It was freezing cold and I thought if I went for a walk up the block it would wake me up. As I was leaving the room, John said, "Hold up, I'm coming with you." I could not believe he came with me. He told me a story about when the Beatles first started out, they used to run away from thugs. Here I am, I'm walking down the street in New York City expecting, "Hey, look at you, you're walking down the street with John Lennon!" I wanted to share it with the world but there was no one on the street at all. But it was a great personal moment for me and I'll never forget it.

Jack Douglas (producer, *Double Fantasy*): "Walking on Thin Ice" was a breakthrough. It was just an idea during the *Double Fantasy* sessions. The song was a loop. We kept looping the same few bars together. John was supposed to go to Bermuda after we finished *Double Fantasy*. And at the time I was doing another project for RCA called Karen Lawrence and the Pinz, kind of a punk thing, and John called me. He said, "Listen, this 'Walking on Thin Ice' idea, I really wanna finish it because it's the one that's really gonna set her off." He thought they'd really made a splash with the *Double Fantasy* album and how that song was really gonna make her career.

He didn't want anybody else at these sessions, which I thought was unusual. It was just the four of us in the room—me, my assistant engineer, Steve Marcantonio, and John and Yoko. I was engineering. John and I played guitars. We did the recording at the Record Plant because I was already there working on a record. Everybody was real excited how the track was turning out. John plays the guitar solo and it's me playing the whammy bar. We were just doing wild things, shaking stuff, looping, and then the spoken word stuff.

December 8, 1980

The day started early for John and Yoko. Renowned photographer Annie Leibovitz arrived in the morning for a photo session, which would produce the iconic and strikingly powerful image of a nude John holding on to a fully clothed Yoko that would later grace the cover of *Rolling Stone*.

David Geffen (Geffen Records): I don't think John really wanted to do very much promotion for the album. I had gotten them to do the cover of *Rolling Stone* and had arranged Annie Leibovitz to shoot that picture. Annie was a friend of mine and that picture became historic.

Annie Leibovitz (photographer): Back in 1970, I was lucky to have spent time photographing John and Yoko for *Rolling Stone*. When I heard that Jann Wenner was doing the *Rolling Stone* interview with John, I asked if I could come along and he agreed to let me go. That early shoot in 1970 really set the tone for how I worked with famous people. It was a Beatle, my God! As eccentric as John and Yoko were, they couldn't have been more normal in the way they related to others. I couldn't believe it. They were really unbelievably down-to-earth people. In retrospect, I understand that Yoko said she was surprised that Jann didn't bring a famous photographer and instead took a young kid and gave her this opportunity. I think her and John liked that a lot.

In late 1980, *Rolling Stone* had another cover with John coming up so I got my second chance to photograph him. But I was told that Jann didn't want Yoko on the cover. There was still some animosity in the air over how the Beatles had broken up and if Yoko was part of that. I had gone earlier to the Dakota to take some pictures of John and Yoko around the apartment. From that first session on December 3, I got a sense of what was happening with them. I knew they were working on a video where John and Yoko were making love. I was very fascinated by that. I also remember seeing the cover to *Double Fantasy*, which was the kiss, and I was really enamored with it. So I was placing all that information in my head. In 1980 it felt like romance was dead. I remember thinking how simple and beautiful that kiss was and I was inspired by it.

I really wanted to do something with them together. But I remembered Jann had told me that he didn't want Yoko on the cover. I knew when I went back for the session on December 8 that I was going to take a simple portrait of John for the cover and then I was gonna try this idea of them together in some kind of embrace. I remember John came to the door in a black leather jacket and he had his hair slicked back. I was thrown a little bit by it. He had that early Beatle look, similar to the way he looked in those photos where he's leaning against the wall in Hamburg. (*Author's note: One of these images was used as the cover shot for John's 1975* Rock 'N' Roll *album.*) In truth, I didn't like that look. I liked his long hair. I thought he was trying to capture something that wasn't there anymore. To me everything was so serious (laughs) and he probably was just playing around and thought it was funny. He was obviously in the mood for a photo shoot. I took some photos of John in the window, some portraits of him holding the guitar, just some simple things.

When I first walked in John pulled me aside and said, "It really means so much to me that Yoko is on the cover, too." So I was doubly conflicted, knowing that Jann didn't want Yoko on the cover. I remember saying to John, "Well, we have to do something extraordinary." Also, I remember being a little nervous, but had elicited from John and Yoko the reassurance that we would do something good. I told them I had this idea where I imagined them both in an embrace naked. John was into it, but Yoko seemed a little reticent. "Oh, I'll just take my shirt off, but I don't want to take my pants off," she said. And I said, "Why don't you leave *everything* on?"

That photograph was taken with them lying on this nice cream-colored carpet in the living room of their apartment in the Dakota. Everything was white, the floor was white, the couch was white. They were lying on the floor and John held her. I don't remember what I was standing on, but I took a Polaroid and John looked at it and was very, very excited. He said, "That's it, that's our relationship!" We knew instantly that it was good. [Annie looks through original frames of the session.] Looking at these frames, the shoot started off with John dressed and then he takes off his clothes. I only shot a roll of film.

In terms of the power of the image, after John's death it took some time to digest it and I'm probably still sorting it out. It was hard to understand that I was there at that moment. I was looking for imagery that was inspired by John and Yoko's love for each other. Because she left her clothes on, he's kind of left looking like he's clinging to her, very vulnerable, and in some way saying good-bye. It's a very powerful image. There's a very beautiful thing that happens with photographs and it's not dissimilar to a song where people feed in what they see into the imagery and it becomes its own story. And what a nice story in retrospect.

I was supposed to see them that night at the Hit Factory and show them the photos and I ended up not going. Then I got a call from Jann Wenner that someone with John's description was taken to Roosevelt Hospital. I went to the hospital and waited through the night in the waiting room and took pictures of the doctor announcing his death. Everyone was in shock. I got the film the next day and sent it over to *Rolling Stone*. When I finally went into the office they were mocking up covers with the head portraits I'd taken of John. I went straight into Jann's office and said, "Jann, I promised John that Yoko would also be on the cover." What's great is Jann immediately changed the cover and used that image of them together. He lost sales in the South. It was taken off the newsstands because they couldn't have seminudity.

Within the week of John's death I went to see Yoko and she was lying in bed in a darkened room in her apartment. I showed her the cover and wanted to make sure she was okay with it. She said, "Do what you want with it" and I was so impressed with that. I've never talked to Yoko since then about that picture. It's an extraordinary gift and I feel very honored that I was there to record that moment. But they made it. It's their picture. I was just lucky enough to be the medium.

One of the strongest types of portraits you can take is a relationship; all the ingredients are already built in. If you're lucky enough to capture the relationship of two people, the weight is off the photographer. You're not having to relate so much to the subject, you get to enjoy and see what two people have happen right in front of you.

To this day, that image of John and Yoko together is probably my most famous photograph. It's bigger than all of us.

•   •   •

Early afternoon found John and Yoko in the first-floor Studio One of-
fices, doing an interview with Dave Sholin of RKO Radio Networks.

Laurie Kaye (scriptwriter and co-interviewer, RKO Radio Networks): Our whole team had to be astrologically approved. We had
to submit all of our birth dates and Yoko's friend Sam Green came
up with the date of December 8, 1980, as the perfect time for the interview. That was always so poignant that that date would be chosen
based on all of our astrological components.

Dave Sholin (national music director and interviewer, RKO Radio
Networks): The team that came with me for the interview was Ron
Hummel, producer and engineer, and Laurie Kaye, who wrote
the script. Bert Keane, the national promotion director for Warner
Brothers Records, which was distributing Geffen Records, was also
there.

We flew from San Francisco and got into New York City late
afternoon, early evening. We got together for dinner and went over
notes and thoughts of what we wanted to cover. I knew we didn't
want to focus on too much Beatles stuff, as that's all been covered,
although John did discuss the group during the interview. Here was
a brand-new album done by someone who dropped out of the music
business for five years just to stay home. There were a lot of things
that we covered in that interview.

There was an Annie Leibovitz photo shoot going on in the
morning. The radio interview was set for one o'clock. We arrived at
the Dakota around a half hour earlier. We did the interview in the
Studio One business office.

Laurie Kaye (scriptwriter and co-interviewer, RKO Radio Networks): It was their private inner sanctum office. I remember that the coffee table was so cool; it had a glass top with wrought-iron snakes wound around the legs.

Dave Sholin (national music director and interviewer, RKO Radio Networks): They asked us to take our shoes off and escorted us in this wonderful room with a white piano and celestial clouds on the ceiling.

Ron Hummel (producer/engineer, RKO Radio Networks): Because this was the interview of a lifetime, I had two machines running in tandem to capture it. This was the predigital era. We used a stereo cassette recorder with a high-quality cassette to tape the interview. We used these tiny little Sony condenser clip-on mics that were the size of a pill to tape John and Yoko individually.

Dave Sholin (national music director and interviewer, RKO Radio Networks): Shortly thereafter, Yoko came into the room. It was just her and it was one o'clock so we started talking, knowing John would show up eventually.

Laurie Kaye (scriptwriter and co-interviewer, RKO Radio Networks): John was late because he was still upstairs doing the Annie Leibovitz photo session.

Ron Hummel (producer/engineer, RKO Radio Networks): We wanted to give Yoko as much interview time in advance so it didn't look like we wanted to push her aside and go to John. We interviewed her for thirty minutes.

Dave Sholin (national music director and interviewer, RKO Radio Networks): Then the door opened up and there was John.

Ron Hummel (producer/engineer, RKO Radio Networks): He saw us doing the interview with Yoko and said, "Sorry to interrupt, folks." (laughs)

Dave Sholin (national music director and interviewer, RKO Radio Networks): He took this little leap, jumped up in the air for a second, extending his arm, kind of a "Hey, folks, I'm here, the show's about to begin!" He apologized for being late. He said, "No one told me the interview even started." John was very friendly and upbeat.

Ron Hummel (producer/engineer, RKO Radio Networks): I didn't know what to expect. Through the years you'd hear all these strange stories about how unusual he was. He was one of the warmest guys I've ever met. He wore tinted amber-colored sunglasses. Once in a while he would drop the glasses to emphasize a certain point he was trying to make.

Dave Sholin (national music director and interviewer, RKO Radio Networks): I felt within a matter of ten minutes after we sat down and talked, it was like John was somebody I'd known forever and Yoko couldn't have been nicer. It was that comfortable. That doesn't happen with every interview.

Ron Hummel (producer/engineer, RKO Radio Networks): He was very animated during the interview. His voice sounded like a little kid, he was talking about things like this was the first time this was happening to him. John was a very intelligent man. He wasn't goofy. He wasn't wacko. He wasn't weird. He seemed very well centered.

Yoko, too. She wasn't this witch lady that you occasionally read about in the press. I felt both were more intelligent than their years.

Dave Sholin (national music director and interviewer, RKO Radio Networks): John and Yoko were both very open during the interview. Early on, I told them, "Is there anything off limits that you don't want to discuss, let me know" and they said, "Absolutely not. Just go ahead." They gave me great stuff.

Ron Hummel (producer/engineer, RKO Radio Networks): We specifically never directed any questions about the Beatles to John. The more we didn't mention the Beatles, the more he started to bring it up. He spoke about "when the Beatles did this . . ." or about how he met Paul.

Laurie Kaye (scriptwriter and co-interviewer, RKO Radio Networks): I remember once making a point that the music on *Double Fantasy* was holistic to the experience of their marriage. He looked at me and said, "Yes, that's it exactly." He did that John Lennon thing where he pushed his glasses down to the bottom of his nose.

Bert Keane (national promotion director, Warner Bros. Records): His son, Sean, and my son, Jack, were the same age, so while the tape was rolling we talked about our boys. We clicked right away. He kidded me about my name "Bert" being the name of a character on *Sesame Street*.

Dave Sholin (national music director and interviewer, RKO Radio Networks): One of the most moving things about the whole experience was seeing the connection between John and Yoko. To sit in that room as they would talk about each other and watch their eye contact, you could feel the magnetism. I know they had their ups and downs in that relationship like everyone in a relationship does. But these were people that are connected and meant to be together. It was pretty powerful. You could feel it in the room. To me, that was one of the things I did not expect.

Ron Hummel (producer/engineer, RKO Radio Networks): In the interview he made it clear that he was nothing without Yoko. He told us, "To show how much I loved her, I gave her a blank check." He told us she had it framed on the wall.

Laurie Kaye (scriptwriter and co-interviewer, RKO Radio Networks): The main thing for me was how much love they had for each other and how excited John was about the new music of the day. He said he went through years and years where he hadn't listened to new music. All of a sudden he was getting turned on to all of this music, like the Clash and the B-52s. That was cool because in later years the B-52s would cite Yoko as a big influence on them.

Dave Sholin (national music director and interviewer, RKO Radio Networks): Over the years, I've been asked if I felt John had some kind of a premonition that he thought he was gonna die. That couldn't be further from the truth. During my interview, he says, "I feel like this is just the beginning, this is just the start of everything." He couldn't have been happier or more upbeat. He couldn't have been more looking forward to the future. He was talking about doing more music.

Ron Hummel (producer/engineer, RKO Radio Networks): The interview lasted about two and a half hours. After the interview was over, I kept the tape rolling till the very end. You can hear John gleefully telling us, "I can't wait to get back on the road, I can't wait to tour."

Ron Hummel (right) shares the last photo of John and Yoko together, taken during the late afternoon on December 8, 1980.

Dave Sholin (national music director and interviewer, RKO Radio Networks): We wrapped the interview around four o'clock. They were thrilled with the way it went.

Ron Hummel (producer/engineer, RKO Radio Networks): We spent about fifteen minutes after the interview was over exchanging gifts, getting photos, and autographs.

Laurie Kaye (scriptwriter and co-interviewer, RKO Radio Networks): What I learned in previous interviews was everyone does a million interviews. You wanted to walk in with a gift that was very meaningful, not necessarily expensive. I knew that John had been a house husband for five years so I had the idea to bring something for Sean. I went to Chinatown in San Francisco and bought one of those green plastic Godzilla wind-up toys that shoots sparks out of its mouth. I also brought Yoko's book, *Grapefruit*. I remember when

I gave Yoko Sean's gift, she was delighted and had this smile on her face like, "Oh my God, what a cool thing to do!" John loved it, as well. He said Sean was gonna go crazy. John was winding up the Godzilla and letting it go up and down the length of the coffee table.

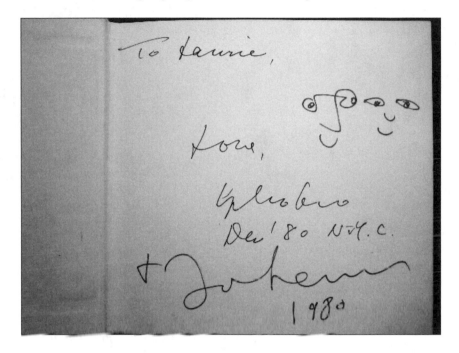

Ron Hummel (producer/engineer, RKO Radio Networks): John and Yoko signed the *Double Fantasy* poster for me. The funny thing was we had a ballpoint pen and this was a poster with high-gloss paper so John was signing it and the pen wasn't working. He tried it two or three times and he almost gave up because they had to leave for the studio. I'm panicking, thinking I'm not gonna get his signature. Finally, Yoko went into another room and got a Magic Marker so he wrote over the top of his signature, "To Ron, love John Lennon." Yoko followed with her signature.

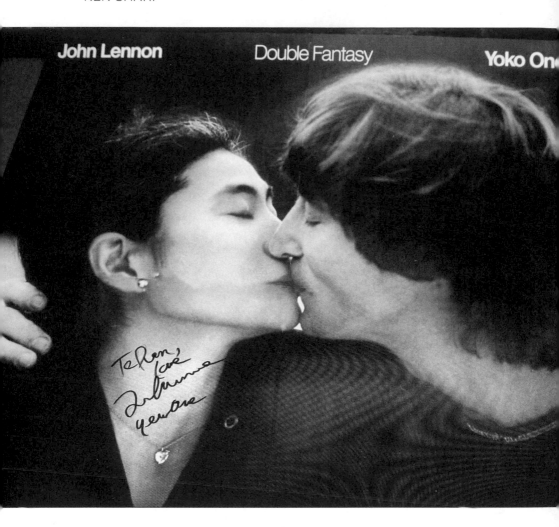

Dave Sholin (national music director and interviewer, RKO Radio Networks): After the interview was over, I had John sign the sleeve of the "Starting Over" single for Debbie, my then-fiancée and now my wife. I told him I'd love it if they would come out to San Francisco and we could all get together and he said, "I would love to do that." John wrote on the single, "Debbie, see you in San Francisco. John Lennon." Bert [Keane], Ron [Hummel], and I took separate photos with John and Yoko.

We had a flight back to San Francisco at six o'clock and we were cutting it close. We went outside to wait for a limo to take us to the airport. Ten minutes later, the limo shows up. Then John and Yoko came out of the Dakota because their car hadn't arrived.

Ron Hummel (producer/engineer, RKO Radio Networks): I remember during the interview, the phone rang several times and it was Yoko's assistant. They were checking about the availability of a car to take them to the studio. I split the channels when I was recording, so when I went back and listened you can hear Yoko going, "Is the car ready? Is it gonna be here?"

John was kind of funny. He was standing outside waving his arms, going, "Where are my fans?" 'cause nobody was really around. Unfortunately, the worst fan possible was there, as we would find out hours later. As we were packing our gear in our limo, this guy approached us and we thought he was just a fan. He asked, "Did you guys interview John Lennon?" He probably saw that we had recording equipment with us. We said, "Yeah, we did, as a matter of fact."

Paul Goresh (photographer): John looked great that day, he reminded me of how he looked back in 1961 in Hamburg, that Teddy Boy look with the Elvis pompadour. He was looking at some proofs of some photos I took of him. Then this guy who'd been hanging around all day approached him to get an autograph on his copy of *Double Fantasy*. I'd talked to him on and off that day. We'd had a terse exchange at one point and then I stopped dealing with him. I sensed he was strange, but I didn't think he was dangerous. He held out the album and a pen toward John and didn't say a word. John said, "Do you want me to sign that?" He took the album and pen and signed it and I took a picture of him doing it. Then John turned back to this guy with his eyebrows raised, "Is that okay?" The guy didn't answer him and backed away. At which point John turned to me and gave me a look as if to say, "So much for that." I'd later discover that was the killer.

Dave Sholin (national music director and interviewer, RKO Radio Networks): John told us, "We're supposed to have a car here to take us to the studio, but it's not here yet, where are you guys headed?" He asked if we could drop them off and said it was on the way.

Ron Hummel (producer/engineer, RKO Radio Networks): We said, "Just hop in the car."

Dave Sholin (national music director and interviewer, RKO Radio Networks): So John and Yoko jumped in and we took them to the Record Plant. I had a great conversation with John on the way over to the studio. I often wished we had the tape rolling.

Ron Hummel (producer/engineer, RKO Radio Networks): I was asking him technical aspects about the album. I thought it sounded so much clearer than some of his other earlier recordings. We also talked about how they did the hand claps on "Starting Over."

Dave Sholin (national music director and interviewer, RKO Radio Networks): We talked a lot about his musical taste. We talked about Elvis, who he loved.

Ron Hummel (producer/engineer, RKO Radio Networks): He called himself "Elvis Orbison" at one point because he was sort of mimicking both of those vocal styles on the "Starting Over" single.

Dave Sholin (national music director and interviewer, RKO Radio Networks): He also talked about Jerry Lee Lewis and Little Richard. And he started singing some of these songs in the car. Then we dropped them off and said good-bye.

•   •   •

Wrapping the RKO Radio interview at 4:00 p.m., John and Yoko's next destination was the Record Plant, where they'd join producer Jack Douglas to finish mixing "Walking on Thin Ice." David Geffen arrives to tell the couple the album has gone gold. Leaving the session around 10:30 p.m., John and Yoko jump into their limo and return to the Dakota, unaware of the unfathomable tragedy that awaits.

John Lennon: "Walking on Thin Ice" was one of Yoko's tracks that we didn't put on [the album] for many, many reasons . . . "Kiss Kiss Kiss" is getting a lot of rock club, new wave, disco exposure. So we made a special kind of disc for them . . . we made a kind of discotheque, long six-minute version of "Walking on Thin Ice" that will go out.[40]

Yoko Ono: The day that John died, I was doing some vocals and then we were mixing "Walking on Thin Ice." I remember when we were mixing it John and I were in the next room and he said, "From now on, we're just gonna do this, it's great!" He really liked the way I put "Walking on Thin Ice" together. He said (excitedly), "Yoko, this is your first number one!"

David Geffen (Geffen Records): I went to the "Walking on Thin Ice" session with Felix Cavaliere of the Young Rascals. Felix had

229

come to see me that day in my apartment. I was his agent. He knew John. I told him I was gonna go over to the studio to see John and Yoko and asked him if he wanted to come and he did. So we went over together. He was telling John and Yoko about how angry he was with Sid Bernstein (*Author's note: former Young Rascals manager*), and of course John had always been angry with Sid Bernstein, who used to make these ridiculous offers to reunite the Beatles. It always used to piss him off. Felix was telling John the story that Sid Bernstein was putting out unreleased tracks from the Young Rascals. John turned to Yoko and said, "Remind me to erase everything in the track, what would happen if I died?" and of course he died that night.

Rabiah Seminole (receptionist, the Record Plant): I'd mentioned to someone that I'd love to have an autograph from John and Yoko. As they were leaving that evening John gave me a little piece of yellow notepaper with their signatures, which also had his and Yoko's caricatures and the date "1980" written on it. I was thrilled. Then I laughingly told him he had misspelled my name and he said, "It's the way it sounds to me, luv." Then I remember watching them walk out the door. This was sometime after 10:30 p.m.

Jack Douglas (producer, *Double Fantasy*): We finished the mix the night of December 8. The plan was to meet at 9:00 a.m. at Sterling Sound to master it.

Steve Marcantonio (engineer, "Walking on Thin Ice" session): I had this whole speech I wanted to give John to tell him how great it was to work with him. He'd just left, so I ran down the hall and barely saw him and Yoko as the elevator doors were closing and said good-bye.

Jack Douglas (producer, *Double Fantasy*): When he was leaving, John had this huge smile on his face. He was wearing a new leather jacket that he'd gotten at The Gap a few weeks earlier. The last thing he said to me was, "See you in the morning."

Rabiah Seminole (receptionist, the Record Plant): Less than thirty minutes later the phone rang and it was David Geffen. He asked if John and Yoko were still there. I told him that they'd left. He said a woman had called him, claiming she was a friend of Yoko's and that John had been shot and was en route to Roosevelt Hospital. I told him, "Hang on, I'll call the hospital." So I put him on hold, called the hospital, and they told me they couldn't release any information. When I got back on the line, there was a woman on the phone and she said David was already on his way to the hospital and that John was dead.

Steve Marcantonio (engineer, "Walking on Thin Ice" session): In my mind I felt it was just a matter of minutes that we found out John had been shot. When we heard the news I thought, That's not possible, they just left.

Rabiah Seminole (receptionist, the Record Plant): It was devastating. I remember one of our recording engineers, Gray Russell, walking out of a session and falling to his knees when he heard the news.

James Ball (assistant mix engineer, *Double Fantasy*): Everybody went into shock.

Rabiah Seminole (receptionist, the Record Plant): Everyone at the studio loved John and we all felt a sense of panic and deep, deep sorrow. We were all crying and the phones were ringing off the hook. Then people started showing up at the studio and they were trying to take the front door off its hinges, which was frightening. Jay Dee Daugherty, one of the musicians who was working at the studio on a Willie Nile session, told me, "You have the last autograph John ever signed."

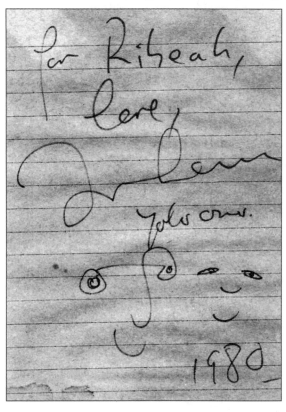

The last autograph John ever signed.

Jack Douglas (producer, *Double Fantasy*): My wife came in and told me John had been shot. We only lived a few blocks away. I thought I was hallucinating for a good six months. I mean, I just flipped out.

Steve Marcantonio (engineer, "Walking on Thin Ice" session): There were four sessions going on in that building that day and every one of them stopped. I had to get the tapes and put them in the tape vault, which was on the roof of the building. I had to climb up on the roof outside into the freezing cold, carrying all those tapes. It was so horrible.

Ron Hummel (producer/engineer, RKO Radio Networks): When we landed in San Francisco we learned that John had been killed. We thought it was a horrible joke. We just dropped him off at the studio. How could he be dead? Because I didn't have a studio at home, I was reduced to clip-leading my tape recorder directly to the phone line to feed bits of audio to our network office in New York so they could start airing snippets of the interview to the radio stations around the country.

The day after, I remember I saw a photo in the paper of his killer. Dave [Sholin] and I spoke on the phone and we said, "That's the guy we saw out in front of the Dakota." Then we realized that this was the guy who must have done it.

Dave Sholin (national music director and interviewer, RKO Radio Networks): The idea was to broadcast John and Yoko's interview around Valentine's Day, February 14, 1981. That was the original plan. We were thinking we had weeks on end to produce an interview special and in light of John's death, it turned out we only had a few days.

Ron Hummel (producer/engineer, RKO Radio Networks): Literally that same night after landing in San Francisco and learning the news of John's death, I left my house and went directly into the production studio to begin putting the radio special together. So, instead of weeks, I had only a couple of days, as the show was already scheduled for air even before production began. The original two-hour show, based on that interview, aired that very weekend across the country. The complete interview was just under three hours and only fifty perfect was ever broadcast. Half of the interview has never been heard to this day.

Paul Goresh (photographer): I didn't know the killer was in the photo I took of John, although I suspected he might be in the background. So I called the New York City police station and said I might have a photo of the killer and they hung up on me two times. Then I called back and spoke to a supervisor and I explained who I was and he said, "Look, you've called here three times. If you call here again, I'm gonna trace this call and we're gonna charge you with hindering an investigation. I got a madhouse going on here, don't bother us again!" and he hung up the phone. Then I called my local police station in North Arlington, New Jersey, and they sent over a sergeant who told me to call one of the New York newspapers. The New York *Daily News* sent a car, took me to their office, and developed the photos in their darkroom. My photo of John signing the album with the killer in the background ran as the front cover of the *Daily News* on December 9, 1980.

Andy Peebles (disc jockey, BBC Radio One): We returned to England to hear the terrible news that John had been killed. A BBC news editor asked me, "Where's the big quote?" and I said, "Just spool through reel six" and we found it. It's the part of the interview where I talked to John about his own security. I don't know to this day what motivated me to do that. When I met with Yoko for the meeting the day before the interview [December 5], there were two big security guards and both were carrying guns. They were quite obviously retired American football players. They were monstrous. You could have parked a Chevy on their shoulders. Because they were around, I'm thinking to myself, I should put a question to John about his own security, and he came out with that extraordinary quote.

John Lennon: I can go right out this door now and go in a restaurant. You want to know how great that is? Or go to the movies? I mean, people come and ask for your autograph or say hi, but they don't bug you, you know . . . "Oh hey, how you doin'? Like your record. . . . How's the baby? Oh, great thanks.[41]

Andy Peebles (disc jockey, BBC Radio One): I can hear him saying it now. He said they won't hassle you and it's great. When the news editor at the BBC heard this, that was the big quote the BBC used. It was an incredible piece of irony and journalistically it was lucky because it became a quote within an instant that went around the world.

Steve Marcantonio (engineer, "Walking on Thin Ice" session): Exactly a week to the day John was killed, we made a montage of snippets of John's dialogue in the studio that was recorded during the *Double Fantasy* sessions. For me, I was still in a state of shock. Seeing Yoko show up in the studio, she had these really big black sunglasses on and several bodyguards, it was very emotional. We spent most of that day putting this montage together for Yoko and that was really tough.

Double Fantasy Redux

Almost thirty years since the release of John and Yoko's *Double Fantasy*, the album remains a revered touchstone for first, second, and third-generation fans and a somber reminder of what could have been.

Yoko Ono: *Double Fantasy* still touches people because everybody experiences the same problems with relationships. John and I were just very human. We didn't pretend about anything. We came out and said, "Relationships are hard, this stuff happens." No relationship is perfect. But people connected with the emotion in songs like "I'm Losing You," "I'm Moving On" and "Give Me Something." It's an honest record.

Jack Douglas (producer, *Double Fantasy*): Like all things Lennon, the album was very honest. The political statement that was being made on the album still stands and it has to do with the relationships between men and women. They were making a bold stand by being so honest. Also, the politics of one world, one people. There's just a lot going on in that record. The one thing where I feel I can take a bow is that I tried to make a record that was timeless in the production values. You wouldn't listen to it years later and say, "Remember that reverb sound?" I stayed away from everything that was gonna make it sound like it was made that month, that year. I always thought John's records sounded timeless, so I wanted this to have that same timeless sound. I still feel when I hear it on the radio that it sounds good. I think John would still be happy with it. I don't think he would want to be redoing any of those tracks.

David Geffen (Geffen Records): I think John Lennon holds a very special place in people's hearts. He did before and he still does.

Earl Slick (guitar, *Double Fantasy*): One of the guys that inspired me to pick up a guitar and do this for a living asked me to play on his record. You couldn't have written that script when I was twelve years old watching the Beatles on *The Ed Sullivan Show*, going, "Yeah, that guy's gonna call me in fifteen, sixteen, and I'm gonna play on a record with him." People would have said, "Yeah, Slick, that's gonna happen, what are you smokin'?" At this point the whole experience seems surreal. Anything that happens in your life that long ago takes on a different edge anyway. And the other thing was, it was the first album John had made in five years and it was a damn good record. I thought it was quite an accomplishment for him. Sometimes when people go away for a while and they come back they're not on their game anymore. And he came back on his game. He was on fire in the studio. He was happy. The whole experience was amazing. We made a great record. Even though I don't see the rest of the guys in the band, there's a bond that will never go away. *Double Fantasy* is simply a great record, that's why it still stands up.

Andy Newmark (drummer, *Double Fantasy*): It's a really good John Lennon record, in which he went back to more of the traditional pop writing, which he was really good at. He wrote really great songs for *Double Fantasy*, memorable songs that people wanted to hear over and over again. I guess one could say that it was quite a commercial record, a record with a very broad appeal. Whatever the magic was in John's best songs over the years, it seemed to be present on *Double Fantasy*. John was totally on the money every day for three months of constant recording. He never let up. To me, it felt like he was back again from being somewhere else for quite a long time, with a renewed enthusiasm for music, and very much at the top of his game . . . happy, healthy, confident, and writing and singing his ass off . . . again!

I was the happiest I had ever been in my life during these sessions. My memory can lapse when it comes to specific details, but not when it comes to my feelings, they are as vivid and clear and real as if it was yesterday. Hugh McCracken is the only person who may have been aware of how I felt throughout this month of recording. I am sure the others did not know what was going on in my head or how much I loved every second of this. My smile is always followed by sadness because he was murdered three months later. All my reactions today to "John stuff" is effected by his being murdered. Little things I remember become more significant than they should, I suppose, and no doubt distorted, as well, by my emotions, because of his death. Every memory I have of him at that time is wonderful and beautiful, but the feeling that comes over me when I think about all those moments is always an all-consuming sadness. I have never been able to shake that feeling off and I do not particularly want to, either. I went from a lifetime high to a lifetime low in three seconds when John was killed. When he was killed, the music in me died, too. It took me two years to climb out of that hole.

Tony Levin (bass, *Double Fantasy*): It was special because John was back . . . but then he was taken from us. That leaves it all the more special, but residing in some emotional realm I don't often visit. For me personally, as for many others, the subsequent years were a rough ride. I wouldn't and couldn't speak publicly about these sessions at all until over a decade later when, in trying to close out a chapter in a book I was writing, I was finally able to confront my feelings about December 1980, feel them fully, and move forward. What makes it a special album? I can't say, but it was a hell of a special album.

Hugh McCracken (guitar, *Double Fantasy*): I hadn't listened to *Double Fantasy* in a long time. I recently put it on and as soon as I started playing it, the tears welled up. It was a real emotional experience for me. There was a lot of joy doing that record. It was happy times and fun times, there was a lot of laughing and joking around. When I hear the songs, I can see John in my mind, working on the tracks. It's the closing musical statement of his life and it's filled with great songs. Listening to the record again brought back the feelings of that period, the joy of the project and the devastation of his passing. Just to be a part of that experience was a gift.

Stan Vincent (Jack Douglas's business partner): This was the rebirth of a man that was coming on like a ninety-mile-an-hour locomotive that couldn't be stopped because of his immense talent and energy. And the songs and the music on the record reflect that. Not only was John so exhilarated by the whole experience of recording *Double Fantasy*, he had a lot of plans. He was writing a Broadway show; Jack and John were planning potentially to build a studio. There were so many amazing projects on the drawing boards. It makes me wanna cry when I reflect on this. He was entering phase three in his career and it was cut short.

Julie Last (assistant engineer, *Double Fantasy*): *Double Fantasy* was his return to music after a long break. He had so much he wanted to share and he was, as he had always been, unflinchingly open and honest. Of course, it was his last finished work and this makes it precious. The terrible sadness is that we will never hear the music he might have made and that we lost someone who tried, with his music and ideas, to change the world for the better.

George Small (keyboards, *Double Fantasy*): This is John Lennon's final artistic and creative statement. Listening to the album again, if you want a model for how a rhythm section should cook, it's all there. The production and performances and the fact that it was a Lennon session makes the album special. Hearing it again, the CD sounds incredible. It's a seminal album and the material will always sound fresh to me.

Jack Douglas (producer, *Double Fantasy*): The "Well" album was our code name for *Double Fantasy*. When you listen to the album, the word "well" comes up a lot. It was our code for where John was at the moment when that record was being made. He was well.

Jon Smith (assistant engineer, *Double Fantasy*): It was a totally new direction for him. After a lifetime of anger and uncertainty, he finally seemed to have found his center. He was totally balanced and confident and it came through in his music. I never heard him speak harshly to anyone, he was willing to listen to other people's ideas and he just seemed very much at peace with himself, Yoko, and the world.

Lee DeCarlo (engineer, *Double Fantasy*): It was a really good record done by a really special guy. Everybody brought their A game and maybe that's why it's timeless. John was one of the guys that held the stick up and said, "If you can jump over this stick, you're good." Jimi Hendrix was another one. Nobody has held the stick up since then.

Ed Rosenblatt (president, Geffen Records): It was a great record. The album still resonates because John was a brilliant artist and I think Yoko has shown over the last twenty-eight years that she's a brilliant artist, as well, not only in her music, but with her influence on many artists and her influence from an avant-garde art stand-point.

Tony Davilio (arranger, *Double Fantasy*): *Double Fantasy* was one of those albums that just caught fire. It was being played a lot on the radio. He was killed while the album was taking off. Perhaps that's another factor why it's still held in such high regard as it was John's last album while he was alive. Had John went on to do more albums, how would it be viewed now? No one knows. But all I know is the songs were great, the production was great, and the playing was great. *Double Fantasy* won a Grammy for Album of the Year and I was given a Grammy as arranger on the album, so the record will always hold a special place in my heart.

Double Exposure
by Roger Farrington

John Lennon was singing as he came down the stairs from his apartment at the Dakota. I sat in Yoko's Studio One office, waiting to meet the Lennons before we would all go to the recording studio. The voice was unmistakable. Amazing, I thought, I'm about to meet John Lennon. The accountant working at a nearby desk looked up at me, smiled, and said, "Here he comes." John Lennon entered dressed all in black—wearing a striking, western-styled shirt—and looked tan, thin, and eager to get to work. As he walked over to shake my hand, he seemed taller than I expected. His long hair streamed down from a wide-brimmed hat. He was carrying a thin briefcase, which I later found out was filled with sheet music for the sessions.

"Right," he said to me, "now who are you?" When I replied, he quipped, "I thought you were one of the accountants. So, you're the photographer, are you? Right, well, do what you've got to do."

Moments after that brief exchange we were off to the Hit Factory. I got one shot of John and Yoko walking hand in hand toward their limousine outside the Dakota. As I backpedaled across the sidewalk, I heard people nearby saying, "Is that John Lennon?"

and "It's John and Yoko."
Someone farther down
the street shouted, "Hi,
John!" and John yelled
hello back. I jumped into
John's green Mercedes
with his assistant and we
followed the limousine.

As we approached the
Hit Factory, which was
really out in the middle
of nowhere, I asked John's
assistant if we could pull
up farther down the street
from the entrance. "If I
can get ahead I'll be able
to get great shots of them
walking into the studio."

The sidewalk was completely deserted all around the Hit Factory; I couldn't believe it . . . no one waiting, no other cameras . . .
totally secret. It kind of freaked me out and I thought that maybe
this is the historic moment that I'm here to document.

As John and Yoko got out of the limousine, I asked them to stop
for a photo. This got them together, walking hand in hand again. I
backed up to get the whole front of the Hit Factory as they walked
under the awning sign. When I made that shot, John was looking
right at the camera and I thought, Wow, that's just what I wanted. I
sort of ducked my head down and followed them through the door.
The security guard was totally poker-faced. I thought, God, this guy
doesn't even know this is John Lennon! We walked straight down
the hall and got right on the elevator and went to the sixth floor. I

couldn't believe that I was actually on the elevator, going up to the recording studio with John and Yoko.

The studio atmosphere was tense, confusing, and at the same time exciting, because this was the *first* day of recording. No one knew what to expect. John and Yoko arrived half an hour or so ahead of the musicians. As we walked into that sixth-floor recording area, I noticed the entryway and adjacent couch. The words "The Hit Factory" hung on the wood-paneled wall. I asked John and Yoko to pause: "Let me just get a quick shot right here." This shot I call my "Windex" shot because there was a bottle of glass cleaner visible on a table (laughs). There was no way I had time to remove the bottle. I had to capture the moment. John made another funny quip, "What, are we here to promote the Hit Factory?"

It was very businesslike and professional in the studio. Many of the musicians and studio staff were gathering for the first time. Technicians were rushing about with equipment that had to be set up and plugged in. It was a whirlwind of activity. Wires began to cover the floor. I had to be careful; I didn't want to trip over anything. And the studio was very dimly lit—all in all, a photographer's nightmare. I just tried to block everything else out and get a couple more shots.

John and Yoko wanted to get to work immediately. Upon entering the studio, John went straight into the recording console and opened his briefcase. Then he walked into the studio, plugged this weird, futuristic-looking guitar into an amp, and started to play. When I offered him a chair and an ashtray, he accepted it with a sincere thank-you, which was nice. John was smoking Gitanes cigarettes, which were very strong, filterless French cigarettes. Yoko had her Nat Sherman cigarettes. I seem to recall that John wasn't playing any particular song, he was just noodling around, experimenting with what kind of sounds could come out of this instrument.

I remember just being amazed by all the incredible different and unusual sounds he was getting. When I tried to get some close-up shots my head was pretty close to his amp and I'll tell you, it was loud! (laughs)

I wanted to get John and Yoko positioned closer for some more photos during my limited time, but John was too absorbed to move from his spot while he was playing the guitar. I remember coaxing Yoko to position herself near her husband.

John Lennon was friendly, open, and humorous, but he was definitely on a mission. He was clearheaded and ready to work, greeting all the musicians around him with open arms. He was full of energy and positivity. Yoko was perhaps more reserved, but confident and in control. When it seemed as though the session was about to truly start, I felt that my presence was intrusive. (At one point, John looked up at one of the arriving musicians—I was probably ten feet away, pointing my camera at them—and he nodded in my direction and said, "This photographer here is me wife's idea." We smiled at each other and I nodded as if to say "good-bye.")

After half an hour in the studio I realized that I should get back to Boston with what I had in the camera. I was under a deadline and thought they needed to send out images to the wire services that day, or the very next day. It was tough to leave the studio, but I knew that if my photos would help announce to the world that John and Yoko were recording again they would be required immediately. Earlier, Yoko asked me if I was going to stay the night and come back the next day. Looking back, I have some regrets not taking her up on the offer. But on the other hand, I felt I had the defining shot of them outside of the Hit Factory, which would be distributed around the world. That photo had the look and the feeling of spontaneity that John and Yoko were looking for.

When I heard the album months later, the song "(Just Like) Starting Over" reminded me of how I felt that first day in the recording studio with John and Yoko. That's what they were doing. That's where all that excitement, energy, and tension came from. Ironically "(Just Like) Starting Over" was the song they recorded the first day. It will always mean a lot to me that I was the first authorized photographer to photograph the Lennons in the recording studio in five years.

• • •

Roger Farrington is a Boston-based freelance photographer whose work has appeared in publications around the world, including Time, Rolling Stone, Vogue, People, Paris Match, *and* Town & Country. *He was the first authorized photographer permitted to shoot images of John and Yoko on the first day of recording their first new album in five years.*

Freeze Frame
by David M. Spindel

I always said it pays to be nice to people and good things will happen. Here's how I came to photograph John Lennon and Yoko Ono in the studio for the *Double Fantasy* sessions. I was in the process of building a new home back in New York and the architect's fiancée said she wanted to be a photographers' agent. I said, "Why don't you come in and I'll tell you all about it." We spent a couple days going over things and when she felt confident, she said, "Now I've got to find a photographer to represent." So I suggested that she represent me. She got very nervous. "How can I represent you? You're a famous photographer, and I've never done this before."

"Cut the crap with the famous photographer," I said. "I'm just a guy who takes pictures and earns a living doing it. I need to give you a chance because if you approach any other photographers, there's no way they're gonna hire you without any experience." So I let her rep me.

It must have been two weeks later that she came back to me and said, "My brother-in-law-to-be got a job working with some musicians recording an album and they're looking for a photographer." I said, "Well, who is it?" And she said, "Well, it's someone who's been in the music industry for a while, but hasn't done a rec-ord in five years." So I asked her again, "Well, who is it?" And she said, "We can't tell you because it's a secret."

I thought to myself that I really didn't want to work with musicians. I did have favorable experiences working with KISS a number of times, but in some other situations it was more aggravation than it was worth. So I figured one way to get out of it would be to put together a portfolio of some photographs that they probably wouldn't like and then they could say, "This guy isn't right for us."

Instead of putting together a portfolio of photographs of KISS and other rock bands I worked with, I put together photographs of some of my very romantic still-life images—things like flowers, antiques, and nostalgia. I also included one shot of a black woman nursing a white baby. It was a very sensitive and emotional kind of picture 'cause that's the kind of work I really enjoy doing. I figured for sure they wouldn't like a photo like that. It turns out that John and Yoko loved it. It was perfect for them because they're very artistic and sensitive to things of that nature. So I heard back that these musicians wanted to hire me, and again not knowing at that point it was John Lennon and Yoko Ono, I still wanted to figure a way to get out of this. So I gave them a price that I thought they wouldn't pay and they said, "Fine." The fee was above and beyond what I believed anyone would charge for a photo session. I told my representative that I wanted a purchase order because who's gonna pay that kind of money? She said, "Don't worry about it, they're good for it." So I said, "I'll take a chance." I love what I do, so how bad could it be?

I went in to do the session in October 1980. I was instructed to go to the Hit Factory. I didn't know that was a recording studio.

I didn't follow music; it wasn't an area of intense interest for me. I enjoyed music, but I didn't follow bands and all that. So I showed up at the Hit Factory and put all my equipment into a little room. I'm sitting there waiting and waiting. It's getting ridiculous. I'm waiting for a half hour, an *hour*, and still nothing was happening. I was getting ready to leave and all of a sudden a woman walks out of the recording booth and she looked familiar, but I couldn't place her. I later found out it was Yoko Ono. She said, "The first thing I'd like for you to take is a group shot." We went into the room where I stored my equipment and I asked her, "So, how many people are in this group?" And she said, "About a dozen people or so." I told her I didn't think they'd all fit in this room and suggested we find a larger place to shoot in the Hit Factory. So I found a reception area with a big couch. I still didn't know who it was I was photographing. Like I said, I didn't recognize Yoko.

So I walked back to where I had left my equipment and there's this guy lying on the floor getting a massage. I thought, boy, these musicians have got it made. Then the guy turns over and it's John Lennon. I got chills, broke out in a cold sweat, and almost had a heart attack, 'cause *him* I knew! He looks at me straight in the eye and jokingly said, "I usually charge people a fee to watch me get a massage," and I said, "Well, I usually charge people a fee to watch me move my equipment, let's just call it even." And he liked that and laughed and said, "I'm gonna enjoy working with you." And that's how I first met John Lennon.

I took the group shot of John and Yoko with their studio band and then Yoko said she wanted some shots of them while they were recording in the studio. Ideally I had brought my strobe lights, but I explained to her that to do this right I didn't feel comfortable taking pictures with a flash going off every couple of seconds. To me it would be a distraction. I told her that I'd like to take photos with available light. Shooting with available light enhanced my photographs because they look natural. Flash can often take away my artistic touch and a certain sensitivity that I work to capture with available light. When you view my photographs of John Lennon it feels like you're standing in the room with him. They're very intimate.

The mood in the studio was very upbeat. John made funny comments throughout the session. He was very personable. You'd see an image of John on TV or in books and magazines and he's this larger-than-life figure. Then when you meet him it was like meeting the guy next door. The fact that he was "John Lennon" was not important. You could tell John didn't let his celebrity get to his head.

Some of my favorite photographs from the session were the ones of John in the three-foot-square soundproof vocal booth. It was very dark, all the lights were out in the studio, and there was just one light above John in the booth. Because it was so dimly lit, to capture the image I just put the camera on the glass of the booth and took the pictures. I couldn't possibly hold the camera still enough and get it sharp because it was so dark and the film I was using wasn't meant for available light. If you look at some of the vocal booth photos there's a slight movement to them. It's because I'm shooting at a slow shutter speed, like a fifteenth of a second. But it all worked to my advantage and the end result of those vocal booth photos captured the essence of him and his music.

When I photographed John in the studio, I'd lean up against the back wall and sort of become part of the wallpaper so I wasn't a distraction. If I wanted close-up shots I'd use a telephoto lens rather than get real close because he was totally involved with doing his music. As a matter of a fact, there's one photo I took of John where he's just sort of daydreaming and drawing cartoons on the console panel with a pencil. As far as I was concerned I was completely oblivious to him, he didn't see me at all. He was in the moment and so was I.

After the session I went back to my studio and developed all the photos. I made enlarged proof sheets and the next day I went up to the Dakota and spent the whole morning with John and Yoko going through the pictures. They were very impressed with my work. I had colorized one of the black-and-white prints and had John and Yoko sign it. It's a close-up of John and Yoko with their faces almost cheek to cheek. Both are wearing sunglasses and looking off into the distance. John made the comment that "we look like Russian generals watching the troops marching by."

When you look at my photographs of John and Yoko, you can clearly see how John was so involved with his music. He loved what he was doing and was totally into it and I feel that's reflected in the photos. It's funny, when John was young and not a star, just a kid playing guitar, I was also just a kid in Brooklyn working in the darkroom in my mother's basement. I was enjoying my hobby and John was enjoying his. Never, in a million years, did I believe I would end up photographing John Lennon.

At the time, I didn't know that photo session would be an important piece of history. I just wanted to do the best I could and capture the feeling and essence of who John was and his music. But the images I captured became historically important when John was tragically killed less than two months later.

What I'm thrilled about most is I'm getting to share the photos with people that haven't seen them. To this day, if I hear any songs from *Double Fantasy*, I feel like I'm back in the studio with them and I get chills all over again.

• • •

Having photographed the likes of Hillary Clinton and Joe DiMaggio, David M. Spindel is an internationally renowned photographer whose work spans the world of entertainment and sports. He was personally selected by John Lennon to photograph one of the last Double Fantasy *recording sessions. His work graces the cover of* John Lennon's Acoustic CD.

Acknowledgments

Putting together a book can be both equally maddening and inspirational. I'm relieved to report that for the most part it was a joy assembling *Starting Over: The Making of John and Yoko's* Double Fantasy. But without the support and friendship of countless people, this book would not have become a reality.

My sincere thanks and gratitude to Yoko Ono for graciously taking part in the project.

Special thanks to Andy Newmark for opening many doors, your continued support and belief in the project helped keep me afloat.

I'd like to express my heartfelt gratitude to Jack Douglas, Tony Davilio, George Small, and Ron Hummel for going above and beyond the call of duty. You guys rock!

Big love to Susan Katila for her faith in the project, delicious homecooked meals, and patience in dealing with the innumerable long hours I was parked in front of the computer.

While my name might be listed on the front cover, the credit for this book should be shared by countless friends, family, and colleagues. I couldn't have done the book without the wonderful support and friendship of the following:

Margie, Tim and Samantha Adamsky, Denny Anderson, James Ball, Jesse Blatt, Rob Bonfiglio, Jim Bullotta, Bun E. Carlos, Robert Christgau, Terri Davilio, Lee DeCarlo, Jack Douglas, Jay Dubin,

ACKNOWLEDGMENTS

Carla Dragotti, Ritchie Fliegler, Mark Ford, Joan and Paul Gansky, David Geffen, Paul Goresh, Bob Gruen, Louis Hirshorn, Robert Hilburn, Bernie Hogya, Jay Jacobs, Arthur Jenkins Jr., Howard Johnson, Bill King, Kevin Lopez, Bob Merlis, Rick Nielsen, Laurie Kaye, Bert Keane, Kip Khouri, Julie Last, Annie Leibovitz, Tony Levin, Chip Madinger, Steve Marcantonio, Hugh McCracken, Charles Shaar Murray, Andy Peebles, Mike Rinaldi, Ed Rosenblatt, Brian R. San Souci, Rabiah Seminole, Carol Sharp, Carol Paula Sharp, Jim Sharp, David Sheff, Kishin Shinoyama, Dave Sholin, Earl Slick, Jon Smith, John Swenson, Eric Troyer, Mary Vicario, Stan Vincent, and Jon Young.

Dave Dunton, my agent par excellence, is owed a standing ovation for his unstinting support and vision and, most importantly, for finding this book a good home.

Jacob Hoye, thanks for your belief in the project.

My editor, Patrick Price, thanks for your help in making this book come alive.

Heartfelt thanks to Jennifer Heddle for racing this book to the finish line.

Much thanks to J. P. Jones for taking care of the copyediting and proofreading.

And of course, I'd be remiss not to salute Roger Farrington and David M. Spindel for your remarkable images that beautifully enhance the backstory behind this wonderful record.

Lastly, a big shoutout to my lovable pooches, Herman, Buddy, and Cha-Cha, for always being there.

Endnotes

All original interviews conducted by the author, except for John Lennon quotations.

John Lennon interview quotations:

1. *Los Angeles Times*/Robert Hilburn, 1980   8
2. *Newsweek*/Barbara Graustark, September 29, 1980   8
3. Dave Sholin/RKO Radio, December 8, 1980   8
4. *Newsweek*/Barbara Graustark, September 29, 1980   9
5. *Los Angeles Times*/Robert Hilburn, 1980   9
6. *Los Angeles Times*/Robert Hilburn, 1980   9
7. Dave Sholin/RKO Radio, December 8, 1980   11
8. BBC Radio One/Andy Peebles, December 6, 1980   11
9. *Newsweek*/Barbara Graustark, September 29, 1980   11
10. BBC Radio One/Andy Peebles, December 6, 1980   22
11. *Los Angeles Times*/Robert Hilburn, 1980   22
12. *Los Angeles Times*/Robert Hilburn, 1980   22
13. *Los Angeles Times*/Robert Hilburn, 1980   24
14. *Los Angeles Times*/Robert Hilburn, 1980   25
15. RKO Radio/Dave Sholin, December 8, 1980   70
16. RKO Radio/Dave Sholin, December 8, 1980   74
17. *Los Angeles Times*/Robert Hilburn, 1980   113

18. *Playboy*/David Sheff, 1980   116
19. *Playboy*/David Sheff, 1980   137
20. BBC Radio One/Andy Peebles, December 6, 1980   144
21. RKO Radio/Dave Sholin, December 8, 1980   144
22. *Rolling Stone*/Jonathan Cott, December 5, 1980   144
23. BBC Radio One, Andy Peebles, December 6, 1980   145
24. *Los Angeles Times*/Robert Hilburn, 1980   145
25. BBC Radio One/Andy Peebles, December 6, 1980   149
26. *Playboy*/David Sheff, 1980   151
27. *Newsweek*/Barbara Graustark, September 29, 1980   154
28. BBC Radio One/Andy Peebles, December 6, 1980   154
29. BBC Radio One/Andy Peebles, December 6, 1980   157
30. *Playboy*/David Sheff, 1980   157
31. BBC Radio Four, 1982   157
32. RKO Radio/Dave Sholin, December 8, 1980   158
33. *Playboy*/David Sheff, 1980   160
34. *Los Angeles Times*/Robert Hilburn, 1980   161
35. *Rolling Stone*/Jonathan Cott, December 5, 1980   164
36. *Playboy*/David Sheff, 1980   168
37. BBC Radio One/Andy Peebles, December 6, 1980   177
38. *Los Angeles Times*/Robert Hilburn, 1980   179
39. RKO Radio/Dave Sholin, December 8, 1980   200
40. BBC Radio One/Andy Peebles, December 6, 1980   229
41. BBC Radio One/Andy Peebles, December 6, 1980   235

Selected Bibliography

Badman, Keith. *The Beatles After the Breakup*. London: Omnibus, 1999.

King, William. *Beatlefan Vols. 1 & 2 1978/79–1980*. Ann Arbor: Pierian Press, 1985.

King, William. *Beatlefan Vols. 3 & 4 1981–1982*. Ann Arbor: Pierian Press, 1986.

Coleman, Ray. *Lennon: The Definitive Biography*. New York: McGraw-Hill, 1984.

Davilio, Tony with Mary Vicario. *The Lennon Sessions*. Canada: Trafford, 2004.

DuNoyer, Paul. *We All Shine On*. New York: HarperCollins, 1997.

Fawcett, Anthony. *One Day at a Time*. New York: Grove, 1976.

Gruen, Bob. *John Lennon: The New York Years*. New York: Stewart, Tabori & Chang, 2005.

Harry, Bill. *The Book of Lennon*. London: Aurum, 1984.

Hilburn, Robert. *Corn Flakes with John Lennon: And Other Tales from a Rock 'n' Roll Life*. New York: Rodale, 2009.

Howlett, Kevin and Mark Lewisohn. *John Lennon Remembered.* London: BBC, 1990.

Lennon, John. *Skywriting by Word of Mouth.* New York: Harper & Row, 1986.

Norman, Philip. *John Lennon: The Life.* New York: Ecco, 2009.

Ono, Yoko. *Memories of John Lennon.* New York: It, 2006.

Peebles, Andy. *The Lennon Tapes—John Lennon and Yoko Ono in Conversation with Andy Peebles 6 December 1980.* London: BBC, 1981.

Robertson, John. *Lennon: A Journey Through John Lennon's Life and Times in Words and Pictures.* London: Omnibus, 1995.

Robertson, John. *The Art & Music of John Lennon.* London: Omnibus, 1990.

Rolling Stone, Editors of. *The Ballad of John and Yoko.* New York: Doubleday, 1982.

Saimaru, Nishi F. *John Lennon: A Family Album.* Tokyo: Fly Communications, 1982.

Sheff, David (Golson, Barry G., ed.). *The Playboy Interviews with John Lennon and Yoko Ono.* New York: Playboy Press, 1981.

Wenner, Jann. *Lennon Remembers.* New York: Fawcett, 1971.

Wiener, Jon. *Come Together: John Lennon in His Time.* New York: Random House, 1984.

Photo Credits